REA
REA

"The unfortunate beauty of this book is that everyone is in dire need of it, whether they know it or not. Forgiveness is not a choice, nor is it a luxury; it is an imperative. We cannot hope to live in peace and freedom unless we learn how to forgive others and ourselves in the once-and-for-all manner that Bruce describes so well."

–*Alan*

"Do I feel differently about forgiveness? YES! I laughed, I cried, I danced, I wrote, I meditated. I stayed on the potter's wheel to let God do more work that had been hidden. A delight, a wonder."

–*Katy*

"Eye opening, profound, and liberating . . . I felt called to actually forgive. I will recommend this to anyone I meet who has trouble forgiving."

–*Steve*

"Seeing a true picture of what forgiveness is—versus what I thought it was—is life changing. I was inspired to forgive. This book can revolutionize the lives of Jesus' followers."

–*Penny*

"Reading this book makes me cry for those who are still tormented by unforgiveness. It is life changing."

–*Sheryl*

"This book will produce enormous life change in anyone with an open heart to the invitation God has for them—freedom."

–*Jennifer*

"This could be the catalyst for a revival. Christ's church is soaking in bitterness, anger, and resentment. A fantastic book that must be widely read."

–*David*

"[This book] has changed how I view relationships. I definitely recommend it."

–*Justin*

"After reading this the first time, I marked my calendar for a 'Forgiveness Retreat' to reread and follow its directions to a tee. Would I recommend this book to others? YES! I think this is a valuable book. A life changer. A culture changer."

–*Ken*

"An unexpected emotional experience. I felt called, convicted, to actually forgive people—even my dad who passed away twenty-six years ago. I will recommend this to anyone I meet who has trouble forgiving."

–*Steve*

"This book is life altering, even if someone only reads it. It is life changing if they actually do it."

–*Cammy*

"I thought I was a good student of forgiveness, but the insights presented by Dr. Wilkinson have caused me to rethink what I believe. I see now that the forgiveness Jesus taught is intense and powerful. I put this book down weeks ago, but I'm still wrestling with what I read. And that's a good thing."

–*Mike*

"As a perfectionist, the person that is sometimes hardest to forgive is myself. Dr. B did a great job helping me to realize that not forgiving myself for sin, or even mistakes, is "a well-disguised root of pride and arrogance deep in my soul." His examples and steps for understanding and forgiving oneself have been life changing."

–Steve

"I did not realize how much weight I was lugging around on my back, and pretending it wasn't there, until I read this book. Unforgiveness is carrying around a backpack of varying weights of painful hurts and brokenness that attracts more weights of pain, making life harder and heavier. Reading this book helped me unload the unforgiving weight I was under, one painful hurt after another. I think regularly now about forgiveness, and take personal stock whether I'm allowing any unforgiveness to creep back into my life's backpack."

–Debbie

"*The Secret of Lasting Forgiveness* is vintage Wilkinson—my favorite since his life-changing book, "Secrets of the Vine." This is a book that will motivate a reader to forgive, as well as show them how."

–Eric

The Secret of Lasting Forgiveness

HOW TO FIND PEACE BY FORGIVING OTHERS AND YOURSELF

Bruce Wilkinson

WITH MARK E. STRONG

z | ZEALbooks

Copyright © 2018 by Bruce Wilkinson

Published by Zeal Books
PO Box 80945
Portland, OR 97280 USA
www.zealbooks.com

Scripture taken from the New King James Version®.
Copyright © 1982, by Thomas Nelson.
Used by permission. All rights reserved

Cover Design: Jason Gabbert
Interior Design: Katherine Lloyd, The Desk
Author Photography: Shannon Bell, Pat Sherman

Originally published under the title: The Freedom Factor:
Finding Peace by Forgiving Others . . . and Yourself

Library of Congress Cataloging-in-Publication Data
Names: Wilkinson, Bruce, author
Title: The secret of lasting forgivness: how to find peace by forgiving others and yourself /Bruce Wilkinson.
Description: Portland: Zeal Books, 2018
Identifiers: LCCN 2018933965 | ISBN 9780999055748 (paperback)
ISBN 9780999055755 (ebook)
ISBN 9781613758403 (audio)
Subjects: LCSH: Spiritual life—Christianity | Christian life.
Classification data is on file with the Library of Congress

Printed in the United States of America

18 19 20 21 22 23 BP   6 5 4 3 2 1

The Secret of Lasting Forgiveness is dedicated to all those who seek the steps to freedom from wounds caused by others or by themselves. May you experience the joy and freedom that only forgiveness can give.

A NOTE FROM THE PUBLISHER

Hi, friends—

You bought this book—or were given it by a friend because you have been wounded by someone in your life and you want to know how to get past the anger and the pain.

We truly believe *The Secret of Lasting Forgiveness* will show you how to find the illusive peace you have been searching for.

And that's why we're offering a money back guarantee.*

We believe that you're holding a book that will change your life.

On to freedom. Jesus is calling.

Don Jacobson Publisher

ⓩ | ZEALbooks

TABLE OF CONTENTS

- PART ONE -
Our Secret Pain

- PART ONE -
Our Path to Peace

PROLOGUE

Dear reader,

In a perfect world, we would talk through the truths in this book over slow cups of coffee in a quiet place. We would laugh together, listen to one another, and possibly even shed some tears. But in the absence of that possibility, I've written this book as a conversation between us.

In these pages, I share my heart, the hearts of others, but most of all, the heart of our good and forgiving God. He loves you. He wants the best for you.

Let's start at the beginning. When God made us, He delicately fashioned something special inside each of our hearts. They were made so that we can experience God's richest blessings, in heaven *and* here on earth.

Our hearts were meant to be open to Him and to others. They were meant for love, joy, and peace. They were meant for freedom, and to bring freedom to our entire being.

So why, for so many of us, do our hearts feel like a locked prison instead of an open door?

Well, our many hurts and wounds batter and warp that door. Eventually, our pain can alter even the shape of the lock until it seems impossible to find the right key. And so our hearts remain closed to the good things of God, closed to freedom. Imprisoned.

And we can forget that freedom is even possible. We forget what our hearts were made for.

But it doesn't have to be that way.

We can all experience God's gifts and life of peace and promise. All that is required is for each of us to open the door of our heart. When we do, His Word promises that joy, peace, and freedom will flood our entire being. It's simple. But not easy.

It's not easy because we often don't know where to find the key that can fit the lock on our hearts.

In the book you are holding, I share a secret. Jesus revealed a key that can revolutionize your life, a powerful key that I have seen unlock the doors of every kind of heart, break the chains of every kind of hurt. Using it will enable you to fling your heart wide open, experiencing the joy, peace, and freedom God made you for—and that He has been longing for you to enjoy fully.

I invite you—journey with me. We'll discover the key that we have searched for far too long. The key to depths of joy and freedom we must experience to believe. So strongly do I believe in this, that if you will commit to reading *and* doing this book, then I will guarantee that you will experience the freedom your heart was made for—a relief from many kinds of pain, and a renewed life of God's freedom.

Oh, *freedom*. It's closer than you think.

Bruce Wilkinson
President, Teach Every Nation

Our Secret Pain

HOW UNFORGIVENESS TORMENTS US

God made your heart for so much—for joy, peace, wholeness, and love. So why does it feel as though those things stay just out of reach?

Something is holding you back—a secret hidden in your heart, a secret that Jesus spoke of long ago. A secret pain, a wound that must be healed.

What is the secret to healing—the key to a life of freedom?

For many of us, one word, from Jesus' lips:

"Forgive."

CHAPTER ONE

The Prison in Our Hearts

HOW UNFORGIVENESS IMPRISONS US

> "Forgiveness is the key that unlocks the door
> of resentment and the handcuffs of hatred.
> It is a power that breaks the chains of bitterness
> and the shackles of selfishness."
>
> —Corrie ten Boom

I t had been a long, weary day for my great-grandmother Lil. She needed a rest.

The only thing preventing her from a nap was the kitchen floor. It was a mess. There was no way she was going to take a needed break with her kitchen floor in a state of disaster. So, already exhausted, she cleaned it.

After scrubbing away that last stain by the old stove, she got off her knees. With a sigh, she rinsed the rag in the sink. As she wrung it, she heard her husband's truck in the driveway—the *clickity-clank* that meant in a few minutes, my happy great-grandpa John would walk through the side door, laughing his way home from work at the steel yard.

It had rained all day. Grandpa John's work boots were caked with mud. And he didn't take them off. As he walked across his wife's clean floor, he left a trail of filthy footprints. He went upstairs, showered, and watched a little television. At dinnertime, he came down to eat.

But he ate alone that night.

His food was on the table, but Lil was missing. He was confused. Still, he ate without her. Bedtime came, but the two went to bed in separate bedrooms without even speaking. The next morning, it happened again. Grandpa John's breakfast was on the table. Grandma Lil was in another room.

As a child, I didn't know about the unseen wall that separated my great-grandparents. Years later, and with kids of my own, I learned the story from my mother over dinner.

"Did you ever see Grandmother Lil and Grandpa John talk?" she asked.

I thought for a moment. "No. Never."

She nodded. "You're right. Neither did anyone else. Because they *didn't*."

I was as shocked as you are, but that's how the story goes. According to my mother, the sole reason for their silence and separation was that Lil never forgave John for walking across her clean floor in his muddy work boots. Although she wiped the mud from the floor that night, the wound that little action opened was never cleansed from her heart. And then my mother dropped the bombshell—"So, how long do you think that they never talked?" My mind was in turmoil. *How long?* "A few weeks?" Then my mother looked at my dad and with a heavy heart said, "Twenty-five years."

Unforgiveness stained their hearts and silenced their marriage for twenty-five years.

As a child, I was oblivious to these dynamics in my great-grandparents' home. I thought nothing about John eating dinner in the kitchen at Thanksgiving while the rest of the family ate in the dining room. I didn't pay much attention to the fact that during Christmastime, he never came in the room with the rest of the family to open gifts. Sure, I noticed that he would sit on the steps, and when the last gift was opened he would go back upstairs. However, nothing seemed strange to me at the time.

For twenty-five years they never enjoyed the warmth of each other's smile, the comfort of each other's embrace, or the other's kiss. They never started the day or went to bed at night hearing the most beautiful words a spouse can hear: *"I love you."* Because of unforgiveness, their life together became painful, sad, and lonely. They lived as prisoners in their own home, but their real prison was inside their own hearts.

My great-grandpa John died before they reconnected. Tragically, Grandma Lil developed a lifelong pattern of unforgiveness, including with her daughter, my grandmother, and numerous others. She filled that little prison in her heart with those around her, one by one.

But I think she was really the one who was not free.

When we do not forgive a person who has hurt us, or if we cannot forgive ourselves for something we have done, we make a prison out of our own heart. The very same heart that should be open to God's joy, peace, and love.

This prison is a dark, painful place. And only true, complete forgiveness can open its doors.

We can always tell when we have imprisoned others or

ourselves. How? Because the pain and darkness of that place always seeps out. It intrudes into our lives. We experience all kinds of painful results, all because of unforgiveness. And freedom can only happen when we open our heart to release the offender from the cell. To let them go. Freedom can only come through forgiveness.

And until we forgive—completely, from our heart—keeping even *one* person in that prison affects the rest of our lives in subtle, tortuous ways we may never connect to their source—our unforgiveness.

Our refusal to forgive others keeps us from joy, peace, and love. And what's more, we are actively made to suffer.

Let me illustrate this with a story.

Several years ago I was speaking at a weekend conference in Atlanta, Georgia. Between sessions, I really wanted a cup of hot coffee. But a line of people were gathering by the wall, waiting to talk privately. That coffee would have to wait.

The next person walking toward me was a tall, lovely woman—very well dressed. Judging from her appearance, she had life figured out. But as she was coming, God communicated to my heart a quiet but specific message. The message was unmistakable. He told me something extremely painful and specific about her past. I was taken aback.

I knew I had no way of knowing on my own what I had just heard, and I felt uncomfortable about what I should do.

She walked up. I chose to simply trust what I had heard, as strange as it seemed. I leaned over when she got to me, and gently whispered, "Are you in trouble?"

She started to weep. She was suicidal, and she quickly confirmed why. In keeping with what I'd heard in my heart—she had had multiple abortions.

My heart ached for her. "I know someone who can help you work your way through this," I said, thinking of a trusted local Christian woman. "I want you to go to her in the morning—will you promise me that you will?"

"Yes," she replied.

I was still concerned, because I felt there wasn't much else I could do to help her at the moment. She promised me that she wouldn't harm herself that night, and that she'd update me the next night on her appointment.

What happened in that appointment set her free. After a few hours of open conversation with my friend, this had-it-together woman realized that her heart was a prison, and that it was *full*. Not only did she need God to forgive her, but she needed to forgive herself as well. She discovered that her desire to end her life was linked with the unforgiveness she held toward herself and those men who had abandoned her. It was all connected.

> Consider—if you took a poll of ten people who were suffering, how many of them would view unforgiveness as a possible cause? Nine? Five? None?

She learned that the force driving her straight to self-destruction was not just guilt, but deep unforgiveness.

But by the end of the conference, it was clear that there was nothing tormenting her soul. She was free, full of peace and joy. It was amazing.

Thinking of it now, I still rejoice in the victory God brought in her life. But I still shudder at the thought of what could have happened if she had not uncovered the connection between unforgiveness and her anguish.

꙳

We are all the same. We live life, vulnerable, often wounded and hurt by others. None of us is made of steel.

When we experience the pain of a deep wound, we are faced with the choice, often very quiet, to forgive or not to forgive. Some of us will choose forgiveness; most will not. At least not without help.

In my decades of ministry, I've heard many, *many* stories of unforgiveness resulting in deep suffering. And one of the great mysteries involves the unexpected ways this sometimes looks. If we were sitting over coffee, I could tell you remarkable stories—like of a woman my wife and I met in Africa, who was healed before our eyes of a painful allergy to fruit. Why did her allergy leave her? Because she forgave her pastor back home in Florida—a man who'd wronged her family deeply. We watched her eat fruit, weeping, for the first time in years, as a result of her forgiveness the night before. I saw it with my own eyes.

Most people don't think in terms of unforgiveness being related to their suffering. I think they haven't made that hidden connection. They might not even have considered that unforgiveness was part of their lives. Many of us see unforgiveness as totally separate, independent from any painful suffering in our lives.

> Have you suspected a hidden connection between unforgiveness and suffering in your life? Not all suffering comes from unforgiveness, but this is an important insight—consider and pray about this connection in your own life.

I've often wondered what would have happened if Grandma Lil and Grandpa John had learned how unforgiveness affected their lives. How much different would those last twenty-five years of their marriage have been? Sadly for them, it's too late in this life. But it's not too late for you.

Wherever you live, whatever your story, no matter what wounds or trauma or hurt is in your past, no matter your age or wealth or social standing—*you still have more life to live*, and God desires it to be abundant, filled with freedom, peace, and joy. You can know the truth, my friend. The truth about forgiveness. And that truth will set you free.

But first there is a secret that must be told—the direct and logical connection between unforgiveness and torment in our lives. Jesus told us this secret in a story that anyone who has read His teachings has seen—though they may have missed it, as I did for many years.

Yes, a secret connection, and the next few pages will give it to you. But I need to warn you—it isn't an easy one.

No, not easy at all.

Just true.

CHAPTER TWO

The Shocking Secret

JESUS' FORGOTTEN STORY OF FORGIVENESS

> "To be a Christian means to forgive the inexcusable
> because God has forgiven the inexcusable in you."
>
> —C. S. Lewis

I was speaking at a large church in South Africa. We met in a huge dome-shaped building, filled with almost five thousand people. I was talking about family dynamics between different generations that day—how parents, children, and grandchildren interact, based upon my book *Experiencing Spiritual Breakthroughs*. I was truly enjoying the day, passionate about my message. I'm not even sure how the topic came up, but I ended up making a brief comment on forgiveness. In my mind, it was a quick detour.

But it was anything but a detour. After mentioning forgiveness, I could feel the tension between adult children and their parents in the audience. It was obvious, painful, and growing. It needed to be addressed. Before I knew it, I heard myself calling them to respond to it. "If you have resentment and unforgiveness toward your parents and have put up walls, if you find yourself often avoiding them and want to break free—please stand. Come forward."

Twenty-five hundred people stood up.

I was in shock as they poured forward. Hundreds of them were weeping quietly. I quickly shot a prayer to God, *Lord, I know how to help one or two people at the same time, but how can I help twenty-five hundred people forgive?*

These people coming to the altar represented hundreds of households, each with a personal story. In some homes, much like Lil and John, entire families rarely talked with each other. In others, the parents were close to divorce and separation. Some were experiencing trauma because of one member's selfishness, abuse, or neglect. Others were ready to give up on God because He didn't seem to be answering their prayers to repair the brokenness and wounds infecting their family for years. Many sons and daughters had left home because of their alienation and hatred for their parents.

It was overwhelming. But healing had to be personal. So I asked these twenty-five hundred people to pick a partner—men with men, women with women. I asked them to face each other so they could help one another forgive. Once they were all paired up and facing one another, I led them step by step through the process of forgiveness.

They named their wounds and their pain. They forgave from the heart—and their hearts broke open. It was magnificent—forgiveness *flooded* the room. Joyful weeping broke out in sobs. The room felt so *peaceful.*

As dramatic as it was to watch, the real drama was happening on the inside—in the hearts of those making the choice to open in forgiveness. Invisible walls of hatred collapsed. Families that had been torn apart were joined once again. Freedom rang out in hearts that had been prisons of unforgiveness only minutes before. Torment left for thousands of households because of one little invitation to forgive.

The church's leaders would tell me later that the congregation had a revival not only in the church but in their homes. The church broke through to a new level of health. Why? Because the underlying cause of their spiritual apathy and pain had been overcome. They forgave others. They forgave themselves. They received God's forgiveness.

And God poured out His blessings in a wonderful way on their opened hearts.

⁂

Friend, unforgiveness is always accompanied by suffering of some kind—it is a universal reality. It affects billions of people.

But at this point, we should be asking some tough questions. If unforgiveness and suffering are indeed connected, then *why*? *Who* controls that connection? *How* does it produce suffering? *What kind of suffering*?

Would you be willing to accept the answers from the greatest teacher—Jesus?

I'll warn you, though—His answer is not going to be what you think.

You may be as shocked as I was when you see it.

When I saw this for the first time many years ago, it was during a period of my life when I was dealing with significant unforgiveness—in hindsight, often without even knowing what I was wrestling with. I was reading in the book of Matthew, studying one of Jesus' parables.

Jesus loved to teach His deepest spiritual truths through stories. A parable is a fictional story that teaches an important truth.

The passage in front of me—Matthew 18:21–35—contained a familiar parable, often titled, "The Unmerciful Servant."

As I read this classic passage that I'd read many times before, a shocking truth leapt out at me. All of a sudden, the *point* of the passage, a point I'd missed while reading this dozens of times, was right in front of me. My eyes widened.

> As you prepare to read through the following story, will you pray this short prayer with me?
>
> *Lord, I want to know the truth about forgiveness. Please teach me by Your Holy Spirit to see my own heart clearly, and let me choose, like You do, the way of forgiveness and freedom. In the name of Jesus, who died so that I could experience His forgiveness for all my sins, Amen.*

Jesus used this story to drive home the main reason why we should forgive those who have hurt us. And that reason is not what we might think.

Read the parable in Matthew 18 with me.

Then Peter came to Him and said, "Lord, how often shall my brother sin against me, and I forgive him? Up to seven times?"

Jesus said to him, "I do not say to you, up to seven times, but up to seventy times seven. Therefore, the kingdom of heaven is like a certain king who wanted to settle accounts with his servants." (vv. 21–23)

In response to a question about how often one should forgive, Jesus gave His disciple Peter a seemingly impossible number—"seventy times seven." He could have left the issue at that.

But Jesus then told a story that revealed *why* Peter should choose to forgive without exception, without limit. Because of what I learned in this parable, unforgiveness became a sin I no longer committed. Jesus' words set me free, and they will do the same for you as well. It's that powerful.

The story begins in a king's business chambers. The fiscal business year is ending and it is time to close the financial books. It is time for the king to be paid the money that his servants owe him.

And when he had begun to settle accounts, one was brought to him who owed him ten thousand talents. But as he was not able to pay, his master commanded that he be sold, with his wife and children and all that he had, and that payment be made. The servant therefore fell down before him, saying, "Master, have patience with me, and I will pay you all." Then the master of that servant was moved with compassion, released him, and forgave him the debt. (vv. 24–27)

Person by person the king calls his staff to settle accounts. But one servant is in deep trouble. He owes the king a massive fortune—ten thousand talents was more than a lifetime's income for many of Jesus' hearers. And the servant knows that he can never repay that debt.

Knowing this, the king orders that the servant, his wife, his children, and all that he owns be sold to help offset the debt. When the servant hears this judgment—his life and family to be dismantled and auctioned away—it hits him like a punch to the gut. His knees buckle. He falls to the floor. He begs the king for mercy, pleading for time, for patience, for *anything* but that harsh sentence.

And the miracle of the story?

Out of his deep compassion, the king forgives him the debt he could never repay.

But Jesus' story wasn't over yet.

But that servant went out and found one of his fellow servants who owed him a hundred denarii; and he laid hands on him and took him by the throat, saying, "Pay me what you owe!" So his fellow servant fell down at his feet and begged him, saying, "Have patience with me, and I will pay you all." And he would not, but went and threw him into prison till he should pay the debt. (vv. 28–30)

The forgiven servant exits the king's presence and finds a fellow servant who owes him money. The sum in question is pocket change compared to the debt just erased by his master. But what is the servant's response? Instead of emulating his master's kind, gracious, forgiving character, the servant abuses and assaults his fellow servant, grabbing him by the throat. He demands every penny.

The man pleads with him for mercy—just as the servant had done a few moments before with his master—but he refuses to give it. This ungrateful servant, forgiven the debt of a lifetime, throws another man into debtor's prison until he pays up his pennies.

But someone saw this great injustice.

So when his fellow servants saw what had been done, they were very grieved, and came and told their master all that had been done. Then his master, after he had called him, said to him, "You wicked servant! I forgave you all that debt because you begged me. Should you not also have had compassion on your fellow servant, just as I had pity on you?" And his master was angry, and delivered him to the torturers until he should pay all that was due to him. (vv. 31–34)

The other members of the king's staff watch this servant's ungrateful act, and their hearts break. Was the second servant's debt legitimate—to the point he could legally be thrown in jail? Yes. But the unmerciful servant's petty demands were so far from the compassion of the king, so far from his kind forgiveness, that a report must be made to the king.

Unsurprisingly, the king is furious. He summons the servant and condemns him for not showing his fellow man the compassion and forgiveness he had been shown.

The king then orders the merciless man who had received abundant mercy to be delivered over to the torturers until the previously forgiven debt should be paid.

A rough story. But Jesus wasn't done telling it yet. In fact, the main point of the story was still yet to be revealed.

What is the connection between unforgiveness and suffering? Jesus tells us.

So My heavenly Father also will do to you if each of you, from his heart, does not forgive his brother his trespasses. (v. 35)

As I read those words, my mouth dropped open in shock.

What is the point of this story—the missing motivation to forgive? Jesus spells it out clearly.

Remember that the point of the parable was to answer Peter's question "How can anyone forgive someone seventy times seven?" Most people assume that Christ's answer to that question is grounded in God's gracious forgiveness toward us. This is true, and it is the backdrop of the whole story. We would love it if Jesus had stopped there, leaving us only with a positive motivation to forgive, and had moved on. But He didn't.

His teaching here is both startling and shocking.

Jesus teaches that the Father will deliver us into suffering if we do not forgive others from our hearts.

What is our liberating truth? Our missing motivation to forgive? The reality that God releases us to suffer if we don't. This work is not cruel, not unloving, but it is real and painful.

Most people harboring unforgiveness know they should

forgive those who have harmed them. But they do not. But what if they saw this motivation—one that would make them run to forgive, rather than to hide and hold their debts in their heart? What if there was a motivation so potent and immediate that we would even stop counting how many times we had been wounded—even beyond seventy times seven?

Why should we forgive everyone for everything? Jesus' teaching is clear: "So My heavenly Father also will do to you . . ."

What does that refer to—from the preceding sentence of the story? The master "delivered him to the torturers."

So our heavenly Father will also do to us. We are shocked to read this.

Why? Under what circumstances would our loving God deliver a person over to the torturers? Jesus gave a direct answer: "So My heavenly Father also will do to you if each of you, from his heart, does not forgive his brother his trespasses."

Hard to miss when you see it. But I didn't see it for years.

The master didn't torture the person but did delegate the torture (creating suffering and distress) to others. God will deliver a person to the torturers if each of us, from our heart, does not forgive our brother (another human being) his trespasses (hurts, wounds, injustices done to us).

The connection couldn't be clearer. If we do not forgive we will surely experience some kind of negative result in our life, a situation that could be described as "torture" or "suffering."

And for how long? "Until he should pay all that was due to him." (Based on the larger context and Christ's point in the parable, this refers to forgiveness, not the original salvation resulting from the canceling of our debt for all our sins. The parable is focused not on salvation but on Peter's question of forgiving others who sin against him.) The implication? That as soon as we forgive, the connected torment is legally canceled.

My head spun as I read an old story for what felt like the first time.

⚜

How could we imagine forgiving others seventy times seven times— a seemingly infinite number? Because we don't want the Father to discipline us by turning us over to the torturers until we do.

What does this mean? That there are always consequences— real and painful consequences—to our unforgiveness. If we think our unforgiveness can be pushed down, hidden, stored away without effect, we are terribly wrong. Its presence delivers us to suffering. And it will never be broken until our hearts open in genuine and complete forgiveness.

When we fail to forgive others and ourselves, God takes away the protection of His peace in our hearts. The implications of that vary widely depending on our circumstances, but are always neg- ative. Because of this, we experience various degrees of distress until we forgive. This is the loving discipline of a Father who does not want His child to live a life contrary to His compassionate character. The unforgiveness we hold toward others is far from what He has done in forgiving each of us. So He acts—allowing discipline to bring us to obedience. To true forgiveness.

And that is the shocking revelation at the heart of Jesus' teaching. It is the Father who assigns suffering to accompany unforgiveness in our lives.

He does that because *He loves us* and wants our good more than He wants our comfort.

Many people resist the idea of God making a link between the sin of unforgiveness and our suffering. After all, how could a loving Father allow torment for His beloved children?

First, this is an issue of discipline, not punishment. He is teaching us, even if it initially seems harsh, that our suffering arises from our unforgiveness. He is doing this to motivate and train us to be like Him—a forgiver!

Second, He has provided a path of escape from all torment caused by our unforgiveness. Unlike punishment, which only ends when the punisher decides that you have suffered enough, the suffering brought by our unforgiveness can end immediately—as soon as we, the "unforgiver," have learned to model our character after God's forgiving nature, releasing all of the trespasses of others from our hearts.

And He is waiting eagerly to grant you complete freedom from that connected torment. Right now.

We are all wounded in our lives. We are hurt, and it is natural to hang on to such wounds as unpaid debts.

But Jesus' parable shows that the issue of forgiveness is not what another person did to you, but what *God* will do to you if you don't forgive them. The choice to be disciplined or not to be disciplined is ours to make, all based upon whether we are willing to turn and offer others the radical love and forgiveness that our King has offered to us. Do we have His loving and gracious character yet? If not, He loves us enough to deliver us into suffering as motivation to change.

This is God's radical revelation—forgive others, so you won't have to undergo painful discipline. Forgive others and yourself so you can live in freedom, joy, and peace.

God does not desire to make us suffer, nor does He take pleasure in watching us suffer. Quite the opposite. It pains Him too. But from His love for us, He is willing to place us into the hands of torturers—not because He wants us to suffer, *but because He wants us to forgive.*

And the moment we do forgive "from the heart" the one who hurt us? The discipline disappears.

There is no need for it anymore.

What is my point? The connection that Jesus makes between

unforgiveness and torture is real. It is not imaginary, symbolic, or abstract. Nor are the words of Jesus an overstatement—this is the universal reality of all who choose not to forgive. From Lil and John to you and me. None of us is excluded.

When I studied this passage for myself over twenty-five years ago, I was shocked by Christ's connection between unforgiveness and suffering. I had read that passage so many times, but missed its message.

But when it finally clicked? *Whatever it takes,* I thought, *I want the torment gone. And I don't ever want this cycle to start again in my life.*

I want to know how to end it.

But before the torment can end, we need to understand how it works.

CHAPTER THREE

Trespasses and Torments

WHY UNFORGIVENESS RESULTS IN OUR TORTURE

"Without forgiveness, life is governed by . . . an
endless cycle of resentment and retaliation."

—ROBERTO ASSAGIOLI

M y wife, Darlene, and I were on a Mediterranean sailboat
trip, following the missionary journeys of the apostle
Paul in the book of Acts. Our ship was beautiful, the
other passengers were great, and the tour company had even
arranged for a doctor to accompany us, in case our group had any
medical needs. We were primed for a fantastic time.

But our doctor wasn't. After she boarded, she discovered she
was sailing with a bunch of Christians—apparently a little detail
that hadn't been mentioned in the arrangements. It obviously
bothered her. She seemed boiling inside, ready for a fight.

That night, Darlene and I sat at the dinner table with a few other couples, eager for a good meal. The doctor walked in, knowing me to be the leader of the tour, and sat right next to me. It was obvious that she was agitated. She began to make it clear to all of us that she was not a follower of Jesus, nor someone who wished to be. In a few minutes she had taken over the conversation and was asking some really challenging questions about Christianity.

Everyone within earshot was watching quietly, expecting me to answer her questions. But I didn't really feel compelled to debate with her. Anyway, the others at our table were answering her questions brilliantly.

But she was eager to engage me. Still agitated in the middle of the discussion, she looked at me. "You're the leader," she said. "What do you think about all this?"

"You have been asking some great questions," I replied. "And these folks have answered every one of them, but you still aren't satisfied. Do you know your problem?" She glared at me as I continued. "You can't believe in Jesus."

"What do you mean I *can't* believe?" she demanded.

"All right," I said, "if you think you can, go right ahead. Believe."

"I can't," she said.

"I know you can't," I replied gently. For the rest of the dinner, the doctor quietly ate her meal, wrestling with what I had said.

The next morning Darlene and I headed to the dining room for breakfast. As we walked up the stairs, the doctor was waiting for me, sitting on the side of the deck.

Her fight face from the previous night was gone. Instead, she looked pained. Her eyes were red-rimmed and fatigued. As we started to talk, she said that our conversation had really bothered her, and that she hadn't been able to sleep. Why, she wanted to know, had I said she was unable to believe?

Instead of replying, I had a question. "Who hurt you so deeply?"

She got defensive. "What does that have to do with my believing?" But as we talked, a heartbreaking story began to trickle out. She grew up with an alcoholic mother who abused her. In rages, her mother would berate her, each careless word battering her heart. She was starved for motherly affection. "My mother has never hugged me in all my life," she said. "It hurt me so badly as a little girl, I would cry myself to sleep."

"Would you say you experience torment in your life?" She looked out into the swelling water. "I never thought about it, but yes. My life is full of it." I nodded.

You'll notice that I asked a particular question to the doctor at this point: "Would you say you experience torment in your life?" This question is an extremely important question that I call the "Unforgiveness Verifier." Since Jesus' story reveals that unforgiveness always results in being delivered to the "torturers," then asking a person if they have experienced torment is the correct protocol to verify that the person's underlying problem indeed is unforgiveness. Over the years, every single person who had unforgiveness agreed with that statement. I've come to the conclusion that the Lord makes the person confirm or deny whether that's true or not so you can serve them with confidence.

Back on the ship, the doctor had a notepad on her lap. I asked her to list all the ways her mother had hurt her. "If you want," I said, "your torment can end. But first you must make that list." She agreed, mentioning that it would probably fill half a page. "It will probably be more like three or four," I replied.

As I walked away and headed up the stairs to the main deck, the source of her suffering seemed obvious. She was dragging along behind her a ball and chain of pain and bitterness, with no hope of escape. She was a wonderful doctor, who understood the intricacies of the body. But she didn't understand her own invisible pain.

ּֽׁיִֽי

I have helped many people move past their unforgiveness. I have never met anyone with both unforgiveness and inner peace. In fact, most of the people I've helped forgive haven't understood how the resulting unforgiveness torment can disturb so many different areas of their life. Once upon a time I didn't understand that either.

It wasn't until I studied the Greek word for *torture* in the Bible that I came to understand how unforgiveness has the potential to distress every area of our lives, even those seemingly disconnected from the source.

Maybe you're wondering, too, what areas of your life could be impacted when you don't forgive? What kind of torment was Jesus talking about when He said the Father will hand us over to experience discipline?

> Does "peaceful" describe your life? Ask yourself a few questions:
> - Would others describe me as a peaceful person?
> - Do I have to work to seem like I have life "together"?
> - All appearances aside, is my inner life tormented?

What exactly did Jesus mean? I began to study everywhere in the Bible the Greek word that Jesus used for "torment" in His parable.

In Matthew 18:34, Jesus shared what the Father did to the unforgiving servant: "And his master was angry, and delivered him to the *torturers* until he should pay all that was due to him" (emphasis added). The word used for "torturers" in these verses is based upon the root Greek word *basanizo* (pronounced "bah-sahn-ID-zoh").

Basanizo means to cause another person distress and suffering. In the New Testament, *basanizo* takes on several meanings depending on the context of the word. The following verses illustrate how widely the word varies.

Depending on the situation, *basanizo*:

1. **Refers to physical suffering (Matt. 8:5–6).**

   Now when Jesus had entered Capernaum, a centurion came to Him, pleading with Him, saying, "Lord, my servant is lying at home paralyzed, dreadfully *tormented.*" (emphasis added)

   In this verse, *basanizo* means physical affliction—the pain of the servant's paralyzing disease.

   While not all physical ailments have a direct spiritual cause, I believe (and have seen) that many people are physically afflicted because of unforgiveness.

   We'd be foolish to assume there is a formula that will compel God to heal everybody all the time, but after forty years of ministering around the world, I'm completely convinced that one of the main reasons many people are suffering physically is due to unforgiveness.

2. **Refers to emotional suffering (2 Pet. 2:7B–8).**

   Lot, who was oppressed by the filthy conduct of the wicked for that righteous man, dwelling among them, *tormented* his righteous soul from day to day by seeing and hearing their lawless deeds. (emphasis added)

   In this usage, *basanizo* refers to emotional suffering. According to Peter, every single day ("day to day") Lot's soul was suffering because of witnessing his godless culture. Likewise, some of the discomfort associated with unforgiveness in our lives is manifested through emotional distress. My great-grandparents spent twenty-five years in loneliness and emotional suffering because of unforgiveness.

3. **Refers to the pain of childbirth (Rev. 12:2).**

Then being with child, she cried out in labor and in *pain* to give birth. (emphasis added)

In this instance, *basanizo* describes the wrenching pain a woman experiences during childbirth. Although the pain of childbearing isn't from unforgiveness, it is a descriptor showing the depth and degree of suffering that this word in the Bible can include.

4. **Refers to eternal torment (Rev. 20:10).**

The devil, who deceived them, was cast into the lake of fire and brimstone where the beast and the false prophet are. And they will be *tormented* day and night forever and ever. (emphasis added)

The fourth and most serious verse I found was Revelation 20:10. Here, *basanizo* represents eternal torment that will never end, for those who oppose the good of all humanity and reject God Himself.

What does all this mean? From this brief look at *basanizo*, we see that it refers to suffering in ways that can painfully affect many different areas of our lives.

Again, don't get me wrong here: obviously, *not all suffering is a consequence of the sin of unforgiveness* (Read John 9:1-12 for a perfect example). But the Bible teaches us that some of the many diverse torments we experience can be. And that should make us pause and think deeply about the implications that our inner reality has for every aspect of our lives.

To illustrate this, here is an e-mail I received not too long ago from a woman I once gave counsel to:

Dear Bruce,

I was thinking about our recent meeting at Denny's. I met with you to tell you how I had prayed, fasted, even taught Bible studies, but still did not understand why God was not answering my prayers about my daughter Christy. I was so frustrated. I had done everything any follower of Jesus could to fix our relationship, but it grew worse and her rebellion against God and me just increased.

When you asked me if I had been unforgiving and rebellious against my parents, I had to answer yes. But I was still offended when you told me to get on a plane the next day, go see my mother, and repent for my rebellion that was now influencing Christy.

To be honest, I wished that I had never opened myself up to you. The only consolation I had was that the look on your face seemed to say, "I can't believe I just told her to do that!"

Anyway, I was upset, but open. Nothing else had worked. And I was desperate. I was ready to stop the pain and exhausting stand-offs. So I followed your advice. I wrote down the ways my mother had hurt me and I followed the steps needed to prepare my heart to forgive my mother and to ask her to forgive me.

I bought a ticket and went to see my mother. I'd be lying if I said it wasn't rough, but I'd had enough of the torment. As we sat across from each other, peering into each other's eyes, I explained why I was there. I took responsibility first, and apologized for how rebellious I had been toward her. I asked her to forgive me for every wound I had inflicted on her.

I said that I loved her, and that I forgave her from my heart for every way she has ever wounded me.

And the freedom and peace I experienced at the moment was absolutely heavenly. I was set free. I felt a lead weight fall from my heart. It freed me to go home and ask my daughter for forgiveness. For the first time I was able to truly release her to Jesus.

Things turned out beautifully—something that only the Lord could do. On my daughter's wedding day, she called me into her room. "Mom," she said, "I want to repent, and ask your forgiveness for my rebellion." I was shocked. She was doing the same thing to me that I did to my mother. When she finished asking me to forgive her, she knelt before me and asked me to bless her. It was a glorious day.

Bruce, thank you for your obedience to confront my heart of unforgiveness. Because you did so, a generational cycle was broken. Many years of possible turmoil and suffering were averted.

There's no doubt—this mother was experiencing all kinds of lingering torment in her life for many years, because of her own unforgiveness toward her mother. Though it may seem obvious to you or me, disconnected from the situation, she didn't see her own broken relationship with her daughter as having anything to do with her own unforgiveness toward her mother from years ago.

I need to make an important point here. We never know initially if unforgiveness is the cause of a specific form of our suffering. There is no straight line that goes from points A to Z for us to follow. But one thing is always true, our unforgiveness always results in some type of negative personal consequence to us.

Spend a few moments reflecting over all parts of your life and identify any area that you sense you are suffering in any way. Remember, our "torment" brought by unforgiveness can result in physical, financial, relational, mental, emotional, or spiritual suffering.

Ask again for God to help reveal any hidden areas of suffering or unforgiveness as you progress. Start to consider if unforgiveness torment could be the cause.

It's a connect-the-dots scenario. We need to identify if we have unforgiveness in our hearts. If we do, we can open our hearts and forgive those who have hurt us. And if the torment leaves? We know that it was associated with unforgiveness, and we walk into a new life of freedom.

But can't God find some other way to walk us through this process of forgiveness, than allowing us to suffer until we forgive? Why does He make His plan so difficult to walk through yet so easy to overlook? There's a biblical reason.

In His parable, Jesus made this point clear: when a person does not forgive, the Father sentences them to discipline. For how long? Until they pay the debt—by forgiving the person who wounded them from the heart. This is a conditional transaction. I would describe it as a legal contract.

The entire context of the parable is within a legal framework, of a king's accounts, judgments, and decrees. And at the conclusion, when the king orders his guards to take the wicked servant to the torturers, that is a legal decree, an order given by the governing power to be carried out in the justice system.

God's decree remains in effect until we forgive. That's why no amount of action or faith, no praying, fasting, or even asking God to stop the suffering, will release you from the torment caused by unforgiveness. God has already decreed that you are to be sentenced to the judgment of discipline *until you forgive*. He is not going to break the contract. You need to cancel it.

Asking God for relief without forgiving is useless, because He has already given you the way out. It simply is not an easy way out. He requires you to act as He acts—to be a forgiver. Through Jesus, God has told us, His servants, that the answer to our suffering is forgiveness. God won't change that decree. It's why that mother and daughter kept drifting further apart, painfully, and why nothing that mother tried could fix things.

Read the following from Hebrews 12:5-7 and ponder these verses about God's discipline of His children.

And you have forgotten the exhortation which speaks to you as to sons:

My son, do not despise the chastening of the Lord, Nor be discouraged when you are rebuked by Him; For whom the Lord loves He chastens, and scourges every son whom He receives.

If you endure chastening, God deals with you as with sons; for what son is there whom a father does not chasten?

Now, consider this question: What is the ultimate reason for God's discipline of us? In light of this passage, do you believe that all of God's action has your good in mind—even if it is painful?

This is a hard teaching by Jesus. But there is good news. You are in control of the legal contract. Your action started it. Your action can end it.

This decree is not intended to sentence you to pain and suffering for life. Instead, God deeply desires that you cancel the contract for Him—because you are the only one who can. God doesn't want you or me to be imprisoned all of our lives by our unforgiveness, like my great-grandmother Lil and John. Nor does He want you to forfeit the blessings that unforgiveness will prevent you from experiencing. This is for your liberation, not your incarceration. He is too good a teacher to do your work for you.

When you and I forgive, the legal contract is terminated *immediately*. The moment we forgive, in that instant, the contract is canceled. Our torment ceases.

Let's turn to one of the most familiar passages in the entire Bible to help us understand more fully. It's the Lord's Prayer, found in Matthew 6:9–15. Jesus told His disciples,

> In this manner, therefore, pray:
> Our Father in heaven,
> Hallowed be Your name.
> Your kingdom come.
> Your will be done
> On earth as it is in heaven.
> Give us this day our daily bread.
> *And forgive us our debts,*
> *As we forgive our debtors.*
> And do not lead us into temptation,
> But deliver us from the evil one.
> For Yours is the kingdom and the power and the glory
> forever. Amen.

For if you forgive men their trespasses, your heavenly Father will also forgive you. But if you do not forgive men their trespasses, neither will your Father forgive your trespasses. (emphasis added)

Look closely at those last italicized words: *"But if you do not forgive men their trespasses, neither will your Father forgive your trespasses."*

Jesus was not pulling any punches. If we don't forgive those who sin against us, God won't forgive us when we sin against Him.

Wait, *what*? Was Jesus saying, "If you don't forgive the accountant that embezzled money from your business, or forgive your spouse for having an affair, you're going to forfeit your eternal forgiveness and be condemned to hell"? No. That's not what He was saying. Eternal salvation from our sins comes from Christ's death on our behalf. It is not related to any work that we do—including forgiving others.

If you have been born again, your eternal life is not in jeopardy. But your temporal life on earth? That's a different story. The consequence for unforgiveness is torment before we die, whereas the consequence for rejecting Christ is torment after we die.

According to Jesus, when we fail to forgive, God has stopped forgiving us. When you fully grasp this truth, it becomes evident that both the Lord's Prayer in Matthew 6 and the parable in Matthew 18 both focus on our forgiveness of others.

Could it be that because of our lack of forgiving others that God has a grievance against us that withholds His forgiving power from our lives? Could it be that all those unforgiven sins are like a stack of legal contracts that God requires us to cancel?

Jesus underscores the utter importance of our forgiveness again in Mark 11:25–26:

And whenever you stand praying, if you have anything against anyone, forgive him, that your Father in heaven may also forgive you your trespasses. But if you do not forgive, neither will your Father in heaven forgive your trespasses.

When God decrees a discipline contract against you or me because of our unforgiveness, it's serious. He removes His peace from us as part of the discipline process intended to turn us back to Him so that we humble ourselves and choose to forgive and end the contract against us. We are made susceptible to many unwanted things in our life because that protection is no longer in place. And not only do we have the difficult task of coping with such painful torments, but we also forfeit so many *blessings* that could be ours. There could be a whole life of His joy, love, and peace, just waiting for our open hearts, but finding no way in.

Let me be very clear about something. Forgiveness is not a silver bullet that can magically solve all of our problems and suffering. The truth is that there's no way to know exactly what suffering is connected to your unforgiveness . . . until you forgive. The truth is also that God calls all of us to be like Him—a forgiver.

None of us can afford to live without answered prayer or God's ongoing forgiveness. And unforgiveness locks the door, shutting out the many good things that our loving Father wishes to lavish upon us.

But there is good news. This does not have to be the story of your life. The contracts can go away—all of them.

Today.

God wants you to have that freedom. He wants you to *know* you are free. And he wants you to experience that freedom. Immediately.

Our Father in heaven is a good Father. He is loving and merciful. He gave His only Son so that He could forgive *everyone* for *everything* that they have ever done wrong. And He expects His forgiven children to then have His character—to do unto others what He has done unto them.

Forgive.

What kind of father would God be if He allowed us to live contrary to His love? The very fact that He tells us to forgive without limit expresses the depth of His love for us. For if we obey and forgive others as He does, He will not have to discipline us for not forgiving—and that's what He wants! Just as the implication of Jesus' story is that the king wanted his servant to extend the mercy that he had been given, God wants us to forgive as often as we are wounded. But if we fail to forgive, He loves us too much to allow us to live in sin and error (Heb. 12:6).

Please hear this loud and clear—though He allows discipline intended to teach and restore us, God Himself does not torture anyone. He is eagerly waiting to nullify that contract, breaking the cause of your torment. However, only you can say the "yes" to make that happen. Only you can choose to open your heart. The choice to be disciplined or not is ours.

We must forgive. And as hard as that may sound, God gives us the grace and power to do that anytime we choose. The moment we forgive we are released. We find freedom.

After a long day of visiting the sites of Paul's missionary journeys, I came back to the ship wondering if I would see the doctor—but she didn't come to dinner. The next morning, however, on the way to breakfast, she was sitting in the same spot as before. This time her eyes were red with tears and I asked her, "How many pages did you end up writing?"

"Two and a half," she admitted.

I sat down. I asked her if she would like to be free. "I think this is why I flew from Australia to be on the ship this week," she said. "I never thought I could be free of the depression and constant anxiety in my heart."

The sun shone. She opened her heart and forgave every single one of those "trespasses" that she had written down. She released her mother from the prison of her heart.

That night, Darlene and I were relaxing in our room. Upstairs was an ice cream machine, and Darlene commented it would be nice to have a bowl. So I made my way up. While I was filling a bowl, in walked the doctor.

How different she looked—radiant. Gone were the lines that had etched her face, the marks of decades of anxiety and pain. Her eyes twinkled and beamed. She looked hopeful. Open. She seemed like a different person, full of peace.

Just then the older couple from our dinner table that first night came in. Either we all had a sweet tooth at the same time, or this was a divine arrangement. "You can believe now, can't you?" I asked the doctor.

With joyful tears filling her eyes, she replied, "Yes, I can believe!"

"Well," I replied, "the perfect couple is right here to introduce you to Jesus."

*

Like our doctor, could it be that you have unknowingly fallen into the hands of tormenters?

Ask yourself these questions:

- Is there anyone I need to forgive?

- Am I experiencing torment?

- Might my pain be a consequence of unforgiveness?

Now, go back to the Lord's Prayer. Take a deep breath, and pray it sincerely, slowly, from your heart. Meditate on its words, remembering that the Father in heaven disciplines the children He loves.

Choose to not live in that pain another moment. In the strength of God's all-sufficient grace, make the choice to forgive those who have hurt you. If you do, you will experience relief. The torment will cease the moment you forgive. You can be free. And life can be sweeter than you imagine.

Yes, you can almost taste it! You can feel the breeze of freedom ever gently blowing across your face. You are longing to open the prison door of your heart so that you can forgive. It's time.

But before we can prepare to take the required steps of forgiveness, we need to ask and answer a key question . . .

How does unforgiveness get into our hearts?

CHAPTER FOUR

The Slide of Unforgiveness

WHY OUR SUFFERING CAN'T STOP ON ITS OWN

"There is a hard law. When an injury is done to us,
we never recover until we forgive."

—ALAN PATON

magine—you're enjoying a picnic at the park. On your way to your family's table, you trip over a rock. You fall to the ground and cut your arm. It bleeds, the wound all gritty with dirt and gravel. Your cousin's at the picnic, though—he's a doctor. Using a first-aid kit from his car, he washes the wound out properly and wraps your arm. Your arm is sore for a few days, but it heals perfectly.

Now stop. Rewind. You fall, your arm is wounded, but just five minute before, your cousin was called to the emergency room and had to leave the park. You brush yourself off, wipe off the blood, and go on with the picnic. *No big deal*, you think. You go home. A few days pass, then a week. Every so often you peek at the wound. It is not healing. In fact, it's getting worse. You start to feel feverish. Your whole arm becomes tender and you begin to feel nauseous. Your wounded arm is now starting to affect your entire body—your entire life. When you go out, or others try to hug you, you turn your body sideways so no one bumps your arm. When someone does, sharp pain shoots through your body. You snap at people close to you, or clam up all together. You don't want to admit it, but you need help. If you are going to heal, the infection needs to go.

If an infection is not removed from a physical wound, it will not heal. And worse, infections always spread without intervention.

If we don't remove the dirt and infection from the wounds in our heart by extending forgiveness, the infection spreads.

> Get ready—you're about to take a journey that requires strength and honesty. Work to keep an open heart as you read the following pages, prayerfully asking if one of these stages of unforgiveness describes where you are with the people who wounded you.

Your heart responds to infection the same way. A heart wound must be cleansed to heal. If it is not, the invisible infection will spread. Eventually, our entire life becomes affected, sometimes in ways we don't fully understand.

THE SLIDE OF UNFORGIVENESS

There are many ways that we are hurt in our lives. We can be harmed by others intentionally or unintentionally. That harm can be physical—a blow, a car accident, perhaps even a gunshot wound or a cut. It can be emotional, financial, or spiritual. We can be betrayed, taken advantage of, lied to. We can be mocked, exploited, swindled, even raped or sexually abused.

But in each case, no matter the nature of that harm or how it came to us, after another person hurts us, there is something now present in our hearts that was not there before—a wound.

When forgiveness is not granted, the wound in your heart always begins to fester. Ponder this—if your heart was never wounded by anyone, would there be a need for you to forgive? No. And, if there is no unforgiveness in your heart, would there be a need for a legal contract and discipline to be administered in your life? No.

Wounds are the beginning of this whole process. Wounds in our hearts are not visible to the natural eye—though their effects on our lives may be. We can't see them like we can see a flesh wound. When we go to school, church, work, or just hang out with friends, we don't have mounds of gauze wrapped around our hearts for everyone to see. But that invisibility doesn't mean the wounds will go away by themselves. They won't. In fact, they can't. Just like a natural wound requires attention to heal, so do inner wounds in your heart.

Such wounds can be very painful. Heart wounds will vary in size and the degree of pain depending on what and who caused it. The closer the emotional and relational tie you have with the person who hurt you, the wider and deeper the resulting wound will be. The more serious the crime and its effects on your life, the wider and deeper as well.

And just like a physical wound, the wounds of our hearts can become infected.

※

Throughout many decades of ministry around the world, I've watched unforgiveness spread in the lives of countless people. I've even felt it in my own. But from my experience, not more than one or two out of a hundred people ever know or consider the secret damage—the hidden connection.

Over those years I've met hundreds of people whose hidden unforgiveness spread. It tainted their relationships, their work, their health, their finances, their ministry, even their relationship with God. Each of these lives bear the infection from a single wound, sometimes a wound as small as a muddy footprint on a clean floor.

What a tragedy.

Untreated infections never stay quarantined. They will always grow and spread, making the future worse, not better. There are universal and predictable stages of the progression of unforgiveness.

Let's look specifically at how the infection of unforgiveness moves from one level in our life to the next. As we do, please prayerfully consider where your own heart might be. Could this be part of your own life?

Listed below are the seven steps of how our heart infection spreads from one level of severity to the next. Think of the person who has wounded you the most, and ask honestly—where are you on the slide of unforgiveness?

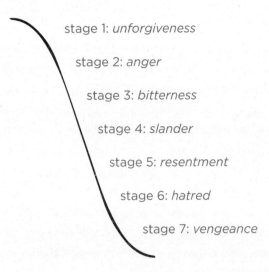

stage 1: *unforgiveness*

stage 2: *anger*

stage 3: *bitterness*

stage 4: *slander*

stage 5: *resentment*

stage 6: *hatred*

stage 7: *vengeance*

Stage 1: Unforgiveness. When you don't forgive, you harbor ill feelings toward the person for their hurtful attitudes or actions. Because of the wounds you experienced by the other person, you decide that you aren't going to forgive them, or maybe you just decide to "forget it" and "move on with your life." You fail to realize that your wound will eventually become infected. And even if you try to ignore it, infection remains. It spreads.

What are the hallmarks of this stage? Putting off true forgiveness by saying something such as that you need to "work through things." Perhaps making a decision to not forgive, or saying no to attempts to reconcile with the person who has wounded you. You hold on to the action that caused the wound, replaying it in your mind. You look for or imagine opportunities to "put the person in their place." You reject or ignore their apologies, if they are offered, or imagine rejecting them if they are offered.

Stage 2: Anger. As time progresses, unforgiveness slides further, causing feelings of anger. When you have been wounded by someone and haven't forgiven them, you will feel displeasure, hostility, and antagonism toward them. Sometimes you even lose your temper toward the person or someone else who simply reminds you of that person. You have to calm yourself when they are nearby because the anger rises. The infection is spreading.

Signs that you are in the anger stage can be obvious—if you tend to manifest anger in ways like yelling, cursing, and overreacting. They can also be subtle, such as being passive-aggressive, backhanded, or even silent toward others. In either case, you are becoming more on edge. Your responses to situations are more and more out of keeping with what is kind and appropriate.

Stage 3: Bitterness. You then begin to have sharp, negative feelings toward the person who hurt you. Your anger may seem to cool and quiet, but you have grown harsh, callous, and untrusting. Your heart toward the other person—sometimes many other people—closes. You are easily irritated and frustrated. You've lost your peace. You no longer trust the person who wounded you, or people like them. You become sullen, withdrawn, and hard. You begin to build protective walls around your heart to keep the person who hurt you completely out of your life.

Are you here? If so, you may recognize yourself when I say that people at this stage don't want to listen to the person who wounded them, can't stand to be around them, and actively work to wall themselves off from them.

Stage 4: Slander. When you reach this stage the infection spreads to your tongue. Slander means to defame or damage the other person's reputation. You begin to gossip and rumor. You talk down about that person who wounded you. You take advantage of any opportunity to swing the conversation around to tearing them down. In your heart, you are glad if you hear they are suffering. If you are still in relationship with them, you constantly misread their motives because you can't trust them. You blame them unfairly, for things not even realistic for them to have done. You hurt their reputation because you have bitterness deeply rooted in your heart.

Your anger and unforgiveness come out of your mouth automatically at this stage, even when you're not consciously thinking about your wound. You volunteer information to people outside or on the fringes of the situation intended to showcase the person who wounded you in the worst possible light.

Stage 5: Resentment. Resentment is a deep-seated cynical attitude toward the person who hurt you. You repeatedly rehearse in your mind all the ways they have wronged you. You keep a hidden list in your mind of all their mistakes and unkind actions—even those directed toward others. You wish the world could see them for "who they really are." You carefully build a whole case in your mind why they cannot be trusted and are unworthy of forgiveness. You link all previous negatives about the person into a well-worn list that grows longer and longer. Your bitterness deepens until you can't think of anything good about that person.

If the person is close to you, you have long forgotten any time that they forgave you or expressed kindness to you. All their good traits are erased from your memory. There is nothing that they do that is right, and nothing they *could* do that is right.

Stage 6: Hatred. At this point, you are working actively to mask the infection, because it has become so ugly that you are unwilling to recognize it in yourself. "I don't hate them," you rationalize, "I just intensely dislike them." Sorry, that's hatred. You are hostile. You avoid the person who wronged you completely. Just the thought of them makes you want to get away. You "really can't stand" the person.

At this stage, you may be unable to hold yourself together in front of third parties or strangers. You may come unglued—your hatred taking your words or actions to a place that you would never have imagined you could go. You are sickened by the sight of the person you hate. Your infection may even be spreading to others, harming relationships far beyond what you would have expected.

Stage 7: Vengeance. When the infection reaches the stage of vengeance, you begin to think or even say things overtly, like, "I want you to pay." You want to get even. You want to hurt them, harm them, humiliate them, and punish them. When you imagine it, you feel better. That inner desire builds to the point where you even consider taking action—you wish them evil (curse them) and you don't want anything good to happen to them (holding back from blessing them). You may wish they were dead—or even want to kill them yourself. This is the most serious stage in the infection. If actions are taken on these impulses, someone is going to suffer.

At this stage, often the infection does spill into action. You are not thinking through the implications of what you do. Others, even innocent people connected to the situation, are themselves hurt and wounded by what you do. In making the person who hurt you suffer, you create misery for many others. And you create tremendous, ongoing misery for yourself.

If you are here, I do not want to minimize the severity of the wound that set you on this slide. But does the process really need to continue? You probably have seen yourself somewhere in these stages.

You may be wondering if unforgiveness has to work its way down that slide from stage one to stage seven. Heart infections are just like physical infections: they inevitably spread. If the unforgiveness has existed in your heart for weeks and months, you have definitely slid to more serious levels. No one can stop this tragic slide as heart infections continue to spread until they are cleansed.

How will you prevent it from spreading more in your own life? If it is not stopped, it will destroy you, keeping you from the freedom and joy you are meant to live.

Fortunately, there is a solution. The Great Physician has a brilliant idea to cure the infection.

In Matthew 18:21, Peter asked the question that sparked Jesus' parable revelation about unforgiveness: "Lord, how often shall my brother sin against me, and I forgive him? Up to seven times?"

I'm sure Peter and the others present assumed the rhetorical question was a good one—and it was. He probably also figured his suggested answer contained a stroke of genius too. After all, seven is God's number of perfection, right? Not this time.

Jesus' answer stunned them all: "I do not say to you, up to seven times, but up to seventy times seven" (v. 22).

There it is. Jesus' brilliant idea.

Forgive your brother or sister seventy times seven times.

Or to put it another way:

God wants and expects you and me to forgive everyone for everything every time.

Initially, this is a hard pill to swallow. At this very moment you may be tempted to close this book.

Don't.

Forgiveness is God's way to set you free from torment and infection. If we forgive everyone for everything, infection can never grow in our hearts. We never will have to undergo discipline because of our unforgiveness. Our hearts will be open and free, and the torturers will have no hold on us.

My prayer for you is that this truth is the sound of fresh hope for you.

Do you hear it? That ring of freedom? That promise of joy, peace, and love?

Good. But do you hear that question behind them too? I do. And it's a big one.

I want to do it, to forgive everyone for everything, from my heart. But . . . how?

I'm about to share the secrets with you. And if you do what Christ teaches, your forgiveness will set you free. Completely free.

Your life will never be the same. Mine surely hasn't been!

Now that you've prayerfully read through the Slide of Unforgiveness, did you recognize yourself in any particular stage? Be sure to have in mind the person who has wounded you most deeply.

Now, on the paper you've used to list suffering in your life, write: "I am at Stage #_____ on the Slide of Unforgiveness."

One last question.

How long do you want to stay here?

PART TWO

Our Path to Peace

THE FORGIVING WAY TO FREEDOM

Through Jesus' parable, we now can see the link between our unforgiveness and torment.

We've seen that God allows this discipline through love, to teach us and compel us to forgive.

We know that He doesn't want us to remain in suffering.

Now it's time to break free.

Forever.

But how? What is the path to peace?

And can we know for sure that we will never be imprisoned by unforgiveness again?

CHAPTER FIVE

Before the Light

PREPARING OUR HEARTS TO FORGIVE

> "The weak can never forgive.
> Forgiveness is the attribute of the strong."
> —MAHATMA GHANDI

One of the most dangerous lies in the world is the idea that our sin comes without consequence. The truth is that every sin can bring tremendous and far-reaching personal suffering. And much of that suffering can be expected because of what the Bible teaches.

The consequences of our unforgiveness are universal. Anyone who persists in unforgiveness will experience torment, though it may appear different depending on our life circumstances. To one degree or another, these consequences are *my* consequences, every time I hold back from forgiveness.

Yours too.

Remember the doctor who found freedom by forgiving her mother? On that same ship was a young man in crisis. He was a crewman, responsible for cleaning the decks and maintaining the sails. During our morning Bible sessions, I would notice him sneaking behind a corner to listen. About midway through our tour, he found me on deck and asked if we could talk.

"Sure," I said.

"It's something personal," he said. "Can we speak privately?"

"Well, are there any private spots on the boat?" I asked.

"Yep," he said. "Up on the sails where I work."

So up we went, higher and higher. I had no idea you could get so close to the clouds on a sailboat.

As I held on to the mast, he said, "My life makes no sense to me, and definitely makes no sense to my parents. It's confusing—I don't know what my problem is. I've been to three colleges, excited at first then dropped or failed out of each. I'd land a job, then either quit or get fired. My folks keep asking, 'Son, what's wrong with you?' I want to succeed. But I always sabotage myself. And the older I get, the worse it is. I don't like older guys like you telling me much of anything. But that Bible stuff you were talking about on deck got me thinking about what my life is becoming. And it's not good."

I listened. "Tell me about your da—" I began. But before I could finish, he was already snapping. "This is about me, not my dad!"

Oh really? I thought.

He was hurt in his heart, hurt so much that he wouldn't let me near his place of unforgiveness. "I know we're talking about you," I said softly. "But this is really about you and your dad—tell me about him."

"He's a big-shot businessman, whose standards I have never been able to meet. If I brought home a report card with four As and a B, he'd yell at me for getting a B. He was always too busy. He never came to one of my ball games or anything I was part of. We never really talk now either. He lives his life, and I live mine. So what in the world does *he* have to do with the way my life is going?"

"It sounds to me like you miss the dad you wish you had," I said.

And up there in the sails, his eyes widened.

❊

Even though he was unable to articulate the process that was occurring in his life, the young man was experiencing what happens to everyone who fails to forgive—a hurt changes *us*.

"Unforgivers" inevitably change for the worse as a person. When an untreated infection resides in your heart, you cannot ever fully recuperate. You will only get worse, as your infection grows more serious.

Let me share another story to illustrate this. (I've changed some details to protect those involved.)

One night, I received a phone call from a couple of board members of a large Christian organization. They were deeply concerned about some negative trends that had been developing over the past two years in their president. Those trends were spreading throughout the organization, jeopardizing their mission.

They were at a crisis, they said. Something must be done. No one knew what had happened, but the president had changed from a leader of integrity, understanding, and kindness into a harsh and dominating person. He had begun to treat people with a dictatorial, condescending attitude. Some key staff had already left in frustration and anger at how they had been treated. If there wasn't a change, they would have to fire the president at the upcoming board meeting. They asked me if I could I fly out to meet with the board and president.

I flew to meet them. I had met the president a few times in the past, but had no idea what had occurred—neither did any other member of the board. After an extended time of prayer, the chairman asked for the board members to share with the president their heartfelt concerns. I listened. The president tried to hide his anger and frustration, but things weren't going well, and we all knew it.

Eventually, it came time for me to join the conversation. I told of my past respect for the president—he had been regarded highly by many. I wondered—if I asked him three questions, would he answer them honestly? He said yes.

My first question was, "Do you sense that this is a critical day in your life and that you are experiencing deep concern from your board—a group of godly men and women—over what has been happening in your life and this ministry?" He agreed soberly.

Next, I asked him, "If it were possible, would you like to return to the person we all know you to be—a man who earned the respect of all who knew you?" This was a much more difficult question. I saw he was on the fence, not knowing whether he did or did not want to change or not. It became so quiet in the room for what seemed an eternity as he wrestled with coming to grips with his intention. Many of the board had their heads lowered as I sensed many prayed for God to intervene. Finally, he quietly spoke, "I don't know if that would be possible, but my family, my ministry team, and I myself wish it could happen. Yes."

"I'm so encouraged," I said. "I believe God will enable us to experience the major breakthrough everyone is hoping and praying will occur. So, here's my final question: Who is the person who wounded you so deeply that you haven't been able to forgive?"

From his immediate reaction, this final question took him totally by surprise. His face twisted in anger and hatred. He nearly yelled: "No one! What a stupid question."

I let this statement hang in the silence, praying for the Spirit of God to open his heart. "Friend," I continued, "you agreed to tell me the truth, regardless of how difficult it was. Who wounded you? What did they do?"

His glare broke. He looked away. We both knew he hadn't been honest yet.

Then he named the executive vice president—who no longer worked there because the president had fired him one late afternoon—and no one knew why or had the courage to ask.

I continued quietly. "So your friend betrayed you?"

He nodded in agreement. "We had been together in college. He was one of my best friends." The story that followed was filled with tragic wounds—everyone around the table could feel his pain and his hatred. It boiled out of him as he shared, just as it had been boiling out for the last two years, poisoning the organization he led.

For the rest of the afternoon, I tried to lead him to forgive his friend. The anger, bitterness, resentment, slander, hatred, and vengeance poured out of his infected heart. He was deeply soul-sick. His personality and leadership had changed as a result as buried and bottled pain had erupted to the surface. Soul sickness and its accompanying torment always transforms us into someone we don't like. And neither do others.

The day was ending. But the strong walls of stubbornness and rebellion in his heart remained strong. We couldn't get it. Finally, at four thirty there was time for just one more attempt. He was so tormented. It was destroying his life, destroying his ministry. Even his marriage was coming into danger. I was overcome.

I stood up and quietly walked to where he sat at the end of the table. I got down on my knees, turning his chair to face me. I reminded him how much God loved him and wanted him to experience victory in this struggle. Then I began to beg him to forgive. Truly—I begged him.

I kept begging him to forgive. The Lord opened my heart. I

felt so much. I began to weep for him. He was shocked, taken off guard—and he broke free. He began to sob. "If this is so important to you," he said, "how can I say no?"

What followed is one of the highlights of my life. Forgiveness flooded the room like a gentle waterfall. Peace broke through. His contract of torment was finally annulled. When he calmed down and composed himself, his real character reappeared. He turned and asked the board if they would forgive him—and then he shared that he would call a ministry-wide meeting the next morning to apologize to everyone.

Years later, I still become emotional, thinking about this. That president and I have become close lifelong friends. God has used this man with a forgiving heart literally around the world. But God's plans for him were almost tragically devastated.

What happened to this leader is the same thing that happened in the young crewman's life. It's what will happen in my life and in your life if we don't forgive. You will slowly but tragically change for the worse. You'll descend down a slide that will take your life to places you never thought you would go, even in your worst nightmare! The Slide of Unforgiveness changes you. The slide reveals the growing negative changes that everyone who doesn't forgive will experience to one degree or another.

Though you may not believe it, there is a positive aspect to this slide. Ask yourself the question, "How have I changed by not forgiving the person who hurt me?" Identify where you are on the slide and choose to get off! You don't have to allow your life to change for the worse in a downward progression. You can exit the slide by forgiving the person who wounded you. When you do, you will find yourself retracing your steps back up the slide until you discover the joy and freedom of loving even those you earlier considered enemies. You then can embrace the peace, joy, and freedom the Father so desperately wants you to have!

Doesn't that sound good to you? However, the slide is not the only way you will change if you don't forgive. There are several other negative characteristics that become a part of our lives when we don't forgive. I wish they weren't a part of the unforgiveness package, but they are. And you need to know them because they could be affecting your life. See how many reflect your life at this point.

HEART HABITS

We are creatures of habits—we all have them. For instance, every morning when I roll out of bed, I stumble to the kitchen to make my morning cup of hot coffee. I then grab my Bible and go to my favorite spot in the house and have my morning devotions. This is one of my good habits—as I'm sure you have a number of good habits too. However, just like we can develop good habits, we can also develop habits that are not so good.

One unhealthy habit a person can develop is the practice of not forgiving others. By failing to forgive just one single person, unforgiveness can eventually become a habitual part of your life, a pattern of living. That habit then transforms into negative characteristics that become ingrained in your life and personality. Here's how you change when unforgiveness becomes a habit:

1. **You develop the habitual response of unforgiveness after being hurt.** Every sin seeks to control a person by becoming a habit. And every habit starts with the first sin. You cannot become an addict without taking a first smoke or first pill. You cannot become an alcoholic without your first drink. You cannot become addicted to pornography without your first peek.

   Unforgiveness is no exception.

   If we don't forgive the first time, we are less likely to forgive the next time.

2. **You fear being hurt again, and build walls around your heart.** Wounds that are not forgiven demand protection from future wounds, like a broken bone that you guard from any contact with a hard cast.

All of us know how to protect our hearts intuitively through two different (but related) strategies: First, we lock the offending person in our hidden heart-prison; second, we seek to protect our heart by building walls around it. You'll learn more about the heart-prison in the next chapter, but let's focus for a moment on those protective walls around our heart.

Here's what can happen to any of us. Does any point sound like you? If so, reflect on it, and write the ones that are true about you on your paper:

- I build walls around my heart to stop people from hurting me.

- My emotions shrivel. I don't feel things like I used to. I keep others from connecting with me, and stop reaching out to them.

- I begin to lose affection and meaningful attachment in my relationships with others.

- I lose emotional sensitivity. I become oblivious to the wounds caused by my aloofness, isolation, and non-emotional engagement. I can only sometimes see this after the fact by the pained response of others.

- I respond to further wounds by fortifying my walls until no one can find an opening to even touch me.

> Each new painful experience only confirms that I should build those walls even higher and thicker. Eventually, everyone is excluded from my life. And I am trapped inside.

Your heart is meant to be alive and thriving. You are meant to feel alive, experiencing all that life has to offer. As too many have discovered, if you build walls to protect yourself from the painful, you have excluded yourself from the joyful.

3. **You mistrust people and misread their actions and their motives.** When a person is filled with unforgiveness, they misread other people. They look at others through eyes clouded with unforgiveness. The more unforgiveness becomes a habit, the more they are easily offended by innocent, normal conversations or situations. Others conclude that you aren't really open to them—and they're right. You can't be open. You are closed. Your heart infection has spread to every area of your life.

4. **You develop feelings of insecurity, along with a poor self-image. Your fear of failure and additional rejection increases dramatically.** Torment is real . . . and increases with additional acts of unforgiveness. That torment includes all kinds of issues with how you view and treat yourself and others.

We cannot help but start feeling insecure with people, as they could eventually wound us as so many others have, so we don't allow them to become close to us. Insecurity reigns. People who struggle with poor self-image often find healing by forgiving others or themselves.

5. **We become passive and fall into a life of self-pity.** We become a "torment victim." Our life isn't turning out the way we thought—but it's certainly not our fault! It's all those terrible people who wounded us—we remember them all. We slide into feeling sorry for ourselves—we see ourselves only as victims of life's unfair and painful realities. We think, *If only I had a fair chance—like those lucky people who have all the breaks in life.* Such people perpetually live with a dark cloud over their head, wallowing in hopelessness and self-pity.

6. **You struggle with anxiety and depression, and you "medicate" to find any amount of comfort.** One way God comforts His children is through His *other* children. When we shut others out, we forfeit love, affection, support, and comfort. Seeking out alternative comfort, many people turn to harmful practices to find relief from their growing anxiety and depression.

    We seek anything that promises to fill our emptiness. We seek escape—drugs, alcoholism, self-mutilation and cutting, habitual over-eating, pornography and one-night sexual affairs, prescription drugs that dull our senses, whatever else that can pretend to fill the void. Even seemingly harmless things become addictive or consuming.

7. **You cannot seem to connect with God and you struggle with loneliness and isolation.** Where do we connect with others? Right—in our hearts! If our heart is walled off, we are going to feel isolated. It affects your relationship with others and your relationship with God. To say it another way, a closed heart keeps you isolated. An open heart allows you to connect with God and others.

Where did it all start—all of this torment, all these habits seeking to destroy our lives, relationships, communities? *Unforgiveness.*

No one anticipates these horrible things to become a part of their life. Have you ever pondered how you would change as a person by developing a habit of not forgiving others? Most of us haven't.

Thankfully, bad habits can be broken.

We just need to develop good ones to replace them.

Let's return to the sailor on the boat.

It was obvious that he had his father locked away in his heart-prison. The first step toward releasing him needed to be compassion—from him toward his father. (We'll cover why this is important for all of us soon.) He needed to see his dad as a human being, separate from the wounding. "I wonder if your dad is lonely for you?" I asked him. "I wonder when he's traveling, if he wishes he had not always been so selfish and unloving—if he'd invested in you as his precious son? And after he yells at you, I wonder if he thinks later on, *Why was I was too hard on my son?*"

He stared at me, and then looked down at the deck.

"Did your dad have a close relationship with his father?" I continued.

"Nah," he said. "His dad was an alcoholic, and he didn't have a relationship at *all* with his dad."

"I wonder if your dad doesn't know how to have a relationship with you?"

His eyes softened. Compassion began to grow, and he opened his heart in forgiveness. God did something special up there in the sails.

Before we came down, I gave him my home address. I told him to write me in a few months and tell me what happened after he went back home after the summer.

Fast-forward a couple of months later when an envelope came from an address I didn't recognize. It was him.

His life had totally changed. He'd gotten off the slide of unforgiveness, and his habits—of life and heart—had changed dramatically.

His letter was full of enthusiasm. "I'm in college," he said. "I'm getting straight As, and I don't have to struggle to stick with it. It's a challenge, but the old urge to just quit is no longer there. It's like it just disappeared. I got a part-time job, and I got a raise after two weeks. My parents are scratching their heads, trying to figure out what in the world happened to me. The pieces of my life have come together."

He had a question, though. "How did you help me to do that when we never talked even for one moment about college or work?"

Now you know the answer, don't you? There was something beneath the surface that was deeply hindering that young man, keeping him from succeeding in college and the marketplace: his relationship to his father. When he forgave, that torment left. He was released to change, to be the person God created him to be.

It may be that you have reached this point and still don't know how in the world you are going to forgive—so deep and traumatic are the wounds against you. Some wounds are so deep, so infected, and so vicious that they may take extra, specialized, or professional care to move through. Extreme cases of abuse, PTSD, mental-health issues, stubborn addictions, or other serious crimes against you shouldn't be faced alone. Remember, forgiveness is not a silver bullet. It is a path to freedom— one that may require some special steps for those who have suffered extreme wounds.

If at any time you find yourself facing thoughts of suicide, self-harm, or violence to others, reaching out for immediate help is essential. God never intended for us to walk some paths alone. Additionally, turning to the professional care of a pastor or trained counselor, preferably with a Christian background, is sometimes essential to fostering the complete work of healing.

Know this—you are not alone.

His story ended so well. And that story can be yours too.

God desires you to live His way instead of your own. He has established the rules that govern all of our lives. He never desired for you to enter the tragic Slide of Unforgiveness but to be like Him—forgiving those who hurt you. As you know, He has repeatedly encouraged you to forgive at various stages of your life. Did you respond to that, or did you close off the communication?

You can see the consequences of closing off to Him now. Are you longing for that freedom? If that young man found freedom through forgiving, can't you? There is no wall too high for that freedom to overcome it through the power of Jesus and the decision that you can make to release wounds and wrongs against you.

But there is an enemy who wants to see your soul enslaved and tormented. And there are lies that can hold you back from walking out.

CHAPTER SIX

The Lies that Blind

LEARNING TO SEE THE WAY FORWARD

"We must develop and maintain
the capacity to forgive."

—MARTIN LUTHER KING JR.

Jesus wants to lead us to a place of peace, of healing—the place where we choose to forgive *from our hearts* others and ourselves for the offenses that have wounded us.

This is real. This is for you.

But there are dangers. Many people begin their walk toward freedom but are stopped by lies or misconceptions that hinder them from the truth. Blinded sometimes by not being able to see what their life will painfully become if unforgiveness is allowed to remain.

There are many lies that try to delay, divert, or diminish our process of forgiving everyone for everything. Let's clear them away. Some of these are specific; some are general. All are dangerous.

Please prayerfully consider each one. Be sure you are free of it before moving to the next.

Be *sure*.

⚘

Lie: "I can't forgive—the person who hurt me is dead."
Truth: Death doesn't bring freedom from unforgiveness. Forgiveness depends only on us.

I'll never forget one woman in her mid-thirties. As a teen, she had been molested repeatedly by her uncle. She had endured tremendous suffering—both from his crimes and from the haunting rage that followed them in her heart. She struggled with self-hatred, leading to destructive behavior, and hated any man who reminded her of her uncle. When her uncle died, she felt relieved for a little while. But it didn't last. After a few months, all the inner turmoil all came back like a raging flood.

She didn't understand that her unforgiveness was not hurting her uncle but herself. Her wound still remained open and infected. Torment remained. Her uncle had died, but his crimes were kept alive through unforgiveness.

Whether a person is dead or alive, if we hold on to unforgiveness, we are the ones who suffer. Not them. Our need to forgive remains, even after the death of one who wounded us. After all, unforgiveness lies in us, not them.

It is our response that makes the difference in our lives. We don't have the power to change what anyone did to us, but we do have the power to choose peace and joy instead of torment. *You have the power, not them.*

⚘

Lie: "I can't forgive until the person who hurt me apologizes and repents."

Truth: Their repentance isn't needed or required in order for you to forgive them.

We all want the truth about wrong done to us acknowledged. We want our offenders to repent and beg for our forgiveness. But that may never happen. So what do we do?

In both Matthew 18 and Luke 6, the Bible doesn't give us a list of preconditions that are requirements for us to forgive others. We are simply to forgive—regardless of apologies or repentance. It is what Jesus has taught us to do. One of the strongest arguments of this is Jesus' example of forgiveness from the cross. "Father, forgive them," He said, "for they do not know what they do" (Luke 23:34). *You don't have to wait for anything to choose freedom through forgiveness.*

Lie: "I don't need to forgive—I don't want a relationship with that person."
Truth: Forgiveness heals your past with that person. The future is a separate issue.

This lie is based on a major misunderstanding about forgiveness. Forgiveness focuses on past wounds, not future relationships.

A tech leader in California had a close friend for many years who served on her corporate board. He even trained her staff. He was a close friend—the CPA for her company, and also in charge of her family's personal finances. She had trusted him for years. So she stopped checking the financial records. Her company went public, with tremendous profit. And her friend vanished. To Europe. With $30 million.

Even if he returned and repented, she would likely never trust him again, with either friendship or money. But she knew she had to forgive the man for his terrible wrong, even though she was soon to begin legal proceedings and was under no obligation to restore him or trust him. *Forgiveness releases the torment from the past but does not require any kind of future relationship.* (The one exception to this is in marriage, where true restoration should be the goal if at all possible. Such cases should be walked through with an experienced and wise pastor, counselor, or other trusted voice who can offer perspective and advocate if there is continuing or serious harm in the relationship.) In my life, some of the people who have wounded me the most, remain as close friends, while others I no longer allow into my life. All are forgiven, but some have proven abusive and untrustworthy even to this day. Don't mistake forgiveness with a required future relationship.

Lie: "I can't forgive because what was done can never be fixed!"

Truth: **Forgiveness is independent of restoration from past wounds even if they continue into the future.**

A pastor friend told me about a courageous lady in his church, whose son had been murdered by a gang member's bullet to the head. She was beyond heartbroken. The pastor shared how she clutched his arm for support as they walked into the hospital and saw her precious boy lying lifeless on a table. He was gone. He could never be restored.

A few months later, she and her pastor walked together into another room—in jail—to talk with her son's killer.

"You took the life of my precious son," she said to his murderer, "who I loved with all of my heart." She went on. "But I forgive you, and because of God's love for me, I love you. My prayer for you is that you would turn your life over to Jesus. God has a plan for you and He can use this horrible situation to work good in your life."

Then, she prayed for God to *bless her son's killer.* She knew things were changed forever with the loss of her son, but she still made the choice to genuinely forgive.

As I write this, my heart is flooded with the faces of person after person who had something so very precious stolen or destroyed by the acts of others—whether on purpose or accidentally. The more irreplaceable the loss, the deeper the wound and more difficult to forgive. All wounds take something away and cause deep loss. Forgiveness is one of the most God-like acts we can ever rise up to embrace. *You can't wait for things to be fixed before you forgive.*

Lie: "I can't forgive. They keep on hurting me."
Truth: Real forgiveness doesn't keep count.

A close friend of thirty years had a wife with a terrible drinking problem. Early in their marriage, she was driving drunk and crashed—with their young kids in the car. Fortunately, no one was seriously hurt. He forgave his wife for her behavior and for endangering their children. She promised it would never happen again.

But it did. Again. And again. He pleaded with her and took her to counselors and treatment centers. But she always fell back in the bottle. One day the police called. There had been an accident. He rushed to the hospital. His wife had been driving drunk again. Their precious children were deeply traumatized. He couldn't forgive her.

We talked numerous times. Finally, my friend saw that forgiveness needed to come again and again, even while ensuring that his wife could never put herself or their kids in peril again. We must understand that we can choose to forgive any and every action. *Forgiveness doesn't mean that there shouldn't be consequences or safeguards going forward.* In the end, his wife lost her driver's license for many years and the judge added other protections for the children.

In Luke 17 Jesus teaches on what to do with a person who repeatedly sins against you but comes back each time seeking your forgiveness:

Take heed to yourselves. If your brother sins against you, rebuke him; and if he repents, forgive him. And if he sins against you seven times in a day, and seven times in a day returns to you, saying, "I repent," you shall forgive him. (vv. 3–4)

Repeated forgiveness is required. Repentance may make our forgiveness easier, but it's not required.

I've found this secret to be quite helpful for me when I am dealing with a person who will repetitively seek to wound me when the opportunity presents itself. I actually practice preemptive forgiveness—forgiving that person before the wound actually occurs. When you continually show love and compassion to the wounding person, he or she will not know how to respond. Not only that, your actions release God to become directly involved in handling that problem for you. And you? You stay free.

Now, there are instances where you need to immediately remove yourself from situations or environments where a person is injuring you, or where the threat of violence or direct harm demands that you or other vulnerable people are protected. Forgiving over and over does not mean you are to subject yourself to harm. You must create healthy boundaries so that you are not a perpetual target of abusive or destructive behavior.

So forgive, but take yourself out of harm's way. Your pastor and church community can be strong supports during the process. Don't try to walk this alone. *Be wise. But don't keep count of how often you forgive.*

Lie: "I can't forgive because I'm suffering for the rest of my life!"

Truth: Your forgiveness can overcome any trespass, even those lasting a lifetime.

She came up during morning break as I was teaching in the African nation of Zambia. "I'm dying of AIDS," she said.

She started weeping, then gained her composure. "I saved myself until marriage and have been faithful all my life. But my husband secretly was sleeping with another woman. He contracted HIV. She even told him she had AIDS, but he never told me, and now I have AIDS. I'm dying. And it feels like my heart died too. My husband *killed* me, and I hate him."

Unimaginable trauma. We spoke about forgiveness in the face of something that, beyond a miracle, could never be made right. "Will God help me forgive him right now? Right here?" she asked me while sobbing.

"Yes," I replied, nodding amidst my tears, and together we experienced God heal her heart as she opened it. Even though she knew she would suffer for the rest of her life and probably die because of her husband's adultery, she chose to forgive.

The consequences of some wounds stretch for lifetimes—even through generations, carrying implications we can never foresee. Can we actually forgive someone, or ourselves, for something of such horrible impact?

Yes. Absolutely.

The painful consequences may continue, but your act of full forgiveness will heal your heart and help you cope with the consequences with grace. The effects of sin may remain, but your inner torment will be gone. The infection can be cleansed. God will heal your heart and give you ongoing strength to deal with the realities that remain. *Nothing is beyond forgiveness, even that which will affect you for the rest of your life.*

⁓

Lie: **"I can't forgive right now. But I will someday."**
Truth: **Forgiveness is best when it happens now.**

This lie is another way of saying, "I won't forgive." Hard, but true.

When is the best time to forgive? At the moment of the wound. In Acts 7:57–60, Stephen was being stoned for his testimony of Jesus Christ. As the rocks from the angry crowd beat against his body, he cried out to God. He didn't ask God for revenge, but for mercy on his killers. "Lord, do not charge them with this sin!" He forgave the people *who were taking his life.* Think about that for a moment.

The best time to forgive is *right now.* Not in the future. And why do you want to wait? Every day you postpone, your torment continues.

Now let's balance that truth. Best is not always what happens. Sometimes, immediate forgiveness really does seem impossible. God is loving. He understands our weaknesses. So it is not a contradiction to this truth to share a prayer that I myself have chosen to use a few times, when a deep and painful wound has made it extremely difficult to cope and forgiving *now* has felt beyond me:

Dear Lord, You know of my pain and trauma. Please grant me a week to cope and I commit to You that I will forgive on or before the seventh day. Please grant me mercy until then.

This doesn't reflect any biblical passage. But I have found through experience that our Lord gives us grace while we prepare our hearts for full forgiveness. *The best time to forgive is now, not later.* The next best time to forgive is within a week, after you have committed to the Lord that you will and then do forgive. Don't allow yourself to continue postponing, because the cost to you is too great.

Do you see the danger of believing these lies? Do you understand the reasons why we should forgive? Would you agree with Jesus that it is absolutely foolish to choose not to?

Knowing this, how can we choose not to forgive?

WHY I CAN CHOOSE TO FORGIVE

We've cleared up some common lies. Now, let's drive our desire for freedom home with a short, but potent, list of reasons why we must forgive. Let's phrase these as truth statements.

> Take the paper you've been taking notes on, and review your list of suffering. Think back to the wounds, to the person who has hurt you the most. Open your heart. When you are ready, read the bolded words below out loud, from your heart.

I can forgive. I will choose to forgive everyone for every wound in every situation because:

1. Jesus has commanded me to forgive . . .

And whenever you stand praying, if you have anything against anyone, forgive him, that your Father in heaven may also forgive you your trespasses. But if you do not forgive, neither will your Father in heaven forgive your trespasses. (Mark 11:25–26)

2. God forgave every sin and mistake I have committed, and He expects me to forgive others . . .

Then his master, after he had called him, said to him, "You wicked servant! I forgave you all that debt because you begged me. Should you not also have had compassion on your fellow servant, just as I had pity on you?" (Matt. 18:32–33)

3. **I have sinned against others and have wanted their forgiveness, and I will do for others what I wish they would do for me . . .**

   And just as you want men to do to you, you also do to them likewise. (Luke 6:31)

4. **I don't want to become a harsh, judgmental person with walls around my heart. I want to be a kind and gentle person . . .**

   Then the master of that servant was moved with compassion, released him, and forgave him the debt. But that servant went out and found one of his fellow servants who owed him a hundred denarii; and he laid hands on him and took him by the throat, saying, "Pay me what you owe!" So his fellow servant fell down at his feet and begged him, saying, "Have patience with me, and I will pay you all." And he would not, but went and threw him into prison till he should pay the debt. (Matt. 18:27–30)

5. **I don't want to continue sinning by going down the Slide of Unforgiveness. I believe Jesus was telling the truth when He said my heavenly Father will deliver me to the tormenters when I fail to forgive others. I want peace and joy in my life.**

CHAPTER SEVEN

Now and Forever

GOD'S REQUIREMENTS
FOR LASTING FORGIVENESS

"Sins cannot be undone, only forgiven."

—Igor Stravinsky

A fter speaking to a diverse group of people on the subject of forgiveness, I was approached by a distinguished-looking middle-aged man. I was making my way out of the room when he stopped me. "Can I have a few minutes of your time?" he asked in a deep baritone.

"I'd be glad to talk," I said.

We moved off the platform for a little quiet in the crowded room. Frustration creased his face. I wondered where this was going—his expression seemed to indicate that his experience conflicted with my talk.

"That was a great talk that you just gave on forgiveness," he said. "It's a subject a lot of people need to hear about."

"Yes, you're right," I said. "All of us suffer wounds in life—

whether by our own actions or from others. And everyone without exception is commanded to forgive others and themselves." As I finished my response, we locked eyes and he nodded.

I had just taught on the parable of the unmerciful servant, saying that once you forgive a person for their trespass against you, the legal contract is void, no longer in force. And, according to Jesus, the torment will cease the moment you forgive from the heart the person who wounded you.

That was his sticking-point. His life seemed to disprove the point. A former close friend and business partner had stolen a large amount of money from their company, hurting his business and family.

"It's impossible for me to forgive this guy just once and be finished with it," he said. "I have to forgive him again and again for the hurt he caused my family and me. And the torment you described comes and goes. So, I'm not really sure you can forgive just once and be done when it comes to forgiving someone who has wrecked your life. I think it is a process that can take a while. In fact, I will probably have to forgive him over and over again until the day I die."

Believe me, I get this. I understand where this man was coming from. It can be extremely difficult to forgive someone who has jeopardized or even ruined your life. It seems to make sense that you may have to forgive them again and again for a single atrocious trespass with ongoing fallout in your life.

But it's my overwhelming conviction that what Jesus teaches is vastly different. Jesus reveals that once you genuinely forgive the person from your heart it is only necessary to forgive once. And it is finished. Nowhere in the Bible does it teach us that we are to repeatedly forgive a person for one incident multiple times. Yes, the Scriptures tell us we are to forgive the person for *every* trespass they committed against us, but these are different infractions. Not the same one over and over.

Why? And what's at stake here? Is there anything wrong with

continuously forgiving a person for the same trespass if it keeps resurfacing?

I believe there is.

Why would you have to forgive someone multiple times? I say this humbly but confidently—because you did not fully forgive. When you *completely* forgive a person, all the proverbial dirt is cleansed from your wound. Once you have removed all of it, your heart will heal. Quickly. There is no need to go back again and again to remove something that is not there. Naturally, if you had an infection in your arm that was not healing, the only reason you would go back to the doctor is to get the rest of the dirt out. But if the dirt is gone you will heal, though it may be sore for a while.

As we stood in that quiet place in the noisy room, I let this man know a truth that I have had to wrestle with—that when we truly forgive, that act of obedience removes all of the dirt from the wound of our heart.

"How can you say you only have to forgive once if you have truly forgiven someone?" he asked.

"Because of what Jesus said in Matthew 18:35," I said. "Jesus put the verb 'to forgive' [Greek, *ahiemi*] in a tense which means you do it *one* time. He could have communicated the essence of forgiveness in a tense that meant 'continually' or 'occasionally,' but He didn't. Jesus says that if we forgive someone "God's way," our wound will heal. We don't have to keep forgiving over and over for the same thing. If we find ourselves still having to forgive someone multiple times for the same thing, we have skipped something, even if we did everything we thought we were supposed to do!"

The man retorted, "But, I did forgive him and really meant it."

So I asked, "What did you forgive him for?"

"Everything, and I meant it," he said.

I said to him, "Okay, if that's the case then you've skipped one of the required steps. Because when the correct steps are followed the contract is terminated and you are free and you'll know by experience you won't need to forgive him again. All torment related to that unforgiveness is immediately halted!"

Keep in mind, however, forgiveness is not the same as dealing with the consequences of that wound. We are commanded to forgive the wounder and then pray for grace and strength to keep handling the consequences of that act. After forgiveness, the focus is no longer on the person who wounded us, but on how to deal with its consequences.

My heart went out to him. I let him know that I'd been in the same place he was now. I told him that before I learned the five requirements for lasting forgiveness, I would have to forgive the same person every time I saw him. However, I said to him, when I learned and followed the requirements that Jesus clearly listed, I was no longer upset inside because the wound had fully healed. I never needed to forgive him again for the previous act.

So I asked him, "Would you like to know the requirements to forgive from the heart?" I could still see by his facial expression and the quick shrug of his shoulders that he had not really bought into what I was saying. He was apprehensive. So in order to help him find the freedom and peace he was desiring, I tried to put him at ease by reminding him that it is impossible for anyone to fulfill the requirements if they don't know them. He agreed. I then said to him, "The same Person who revealed the shocking reason for forgiving is the same Person who reveals the requirements to obtain lasting forgiveness."

This idea perked up his interest, so he asked, "What are those requirements?"

I answered by telling him, "There are five requirements given by Jesus that, if you follow, will remove the dirt from the wound once and for all! Would you like me to share those life-changing requirements with you?"

Without hesitation or any reservation, he responded, "Of course!"

"Great!" I knew he was very close to settling some deep forgiveness issues in his heart, so I shared with him the requirements given by Jesus.

It's time to reveal what it takes to actually forgive. But first, we need to talk about a concept called "protocol"—a specific process for something important, such as the ways that everyday people are expected to interact with heads of state. The person of authority communicates the required rules for the relationship to be acceptable. God does the same thing—establishing patterns that reveal His desire to know and be known, but also revealing that there are right and wrong ways for us to walk with Him.

We may know we need to forgive. We may choose it too. And mean it. But we have to do it God's way to be sure He has accepted our act of forgiveness and then canceled the assigned torment. If we invent our own protocol, even with good motives, we're in for trouble. At the very least, we won't be able to have confidence that we have truly canceled the contract with the tormenters because we met God's universal requirements.

What must we do? What steps does God require?

Prepare to read the five requirements that are integral to true forgiveness. Follow them exactly and your forgiveness will be complete.

THE FIVE REQUIREMENTS OF FORGIVENESS

When I first discovered that God would "deliver me to the torturers" unless I forgave everyone of everything, my life changed. No longer could I look at forgiveness as something of little importance. No longer could I just keep those feelings bottled up, stuffed away. Instead, I desperately sought for God's way, for thorough and complete forgiveness.

After studying what God meant by "torment," I recognized all kinds of warning signals going off in my personal life. I started making those all-important connections between my suffering and my unforgiveness. Connections that I had never thought of before.

Then feelings of powerlessness swept over me. I realized I had absolutely no control over the decision to stop the legal contract of being "delivered over to the torturers." None. God decreed that from His throne in heaven; only God could cancel that decree.

I found myself wishing I had known this powerful truth much earlier in my life—how different things could have been. But my regret didn't change anything except pushing me down deeper into despair.

So as I sat at my desk, I sat back and wondered, "How can I be sure that God would cancel my torment?" Minutes later, I reasoned, "Well, God certainly doesn't want this to be happening to me, so He must have revealed His protocol, His divine requirements, for my freedom." Of course!

Then I returned to Matthew 18 with the assurance that hidden in all those verses must be the answer. Over and over again I read those verses, studying every word to find the answer. Before long, I had written on my notes the five specific requirements that Jesus revealed. Then I checked everywhere in the Bible that forgiveness was discussed and discovered Matthew 18 had all of them. Five steps in black and white. They always had been there, but somehow they never registered in me as they did now.

The despair I was feeling started dissipating rapidly like rain off of a roof. My heart became excited because I realized if I followed those five steps precisely, then I would meet all of God's requirements. And when I did, then He would not only forgive me for my own sin of unforgiveness but also cancel the contract immediately. Jesus' words "until he should pay all that was due to him" set me free. When I met God's five requirements, then I would be freed. Immediately.

This chapter is the first of three very important chapters, the heart of this book. You will now learn what God requires of you in order to forgive to His satisfaction. In the next chapter I'll guide you through each of those steps as you forgive others who wounded you. In the third chapter, I'll guide you to forgive the one person that some find the hardest to forgive—yourself.

May I give a word of encouragement and assurance as we move forward? These five steps work for everyone, everywhere, without one exception. From individuals and couples and families around the world, to churches, to organizations, to warring tribes in Uganda, to alienated denominations in the United States and South Africa, to powerful national leaders in Swaziland, to racial conflict between white farmers and black workers in Namibia, I have seen the unstoppable power of forgiveness breakthrough in every single situation. Follow these five steps, my friend, and you will discover life without torment!

Requirement 1: Open your heart to forgive.

So My Heavenly Father also will do to you if each of you, from his heart, does not forgive his brother his trespasses. (Matt. 18:35)

Jesus tells us to start where the problem of unforgiveness begins—the heart.

Forgiving from our "head"—just thinking the thoughts—isn't true forgiveness. Neither is forcing ourselves to choose forgiveness, forgiving from the "will." Only forgiving from the heart is powerful enough to end our torment. Why? Because you were not hurt in your will or mind, at least not centrally.

You were hurt in your *heart*.

That's where the infection breeds. That's what is festering. That's what needs healing. To open it requires your head and your will too, but the first step is to open up your heart.

When we have a wound, we protect it. We do the same with our heart. When our heart is wounded by someone else or even by ourselves, our immediate response is self-protection. We retreat, building walls and defenses. The problem is that we lock our torment in with us, so our defenses are worse than useless. What we built as a fortress becomes a prison.

But we have the power; we hold the key. We are in control of our hearts.

Before we go further, think of the person who has wounded you the most. What is their first name? Write it on your private notes for this process.

Are you beginning to think about opening your heart toward that person? It's time. In the next chapter, I'll guide you through a process that will help you to open your heart.

Requirement 2: Extend compassion to the person who wounded you.

The servant therefore fell down before him, saying, "Master, have patience with me, and I will pay you all." Then the master of that servant was moved with compassion, *released him, and forgave him the debt. . . .* Should you not also have had compassion *on your fellow servant,* just as I had pity on you? *(vv. 26–27, 33, emphasis added)*

Compassion is the door to forgiveness. Compassion has the unique ability to soften and open a heart that is closed.

Jesus reveals two kinds of compassion. The first type of compassion is when someone else opens your heart for you. When another person humbles himself and asks for mercy and forgiveness, that action can immediately open your heart without any action or determination on your part. Look what the servant did when he discovered the consequences while facing his master: "The servant therefore fell down before him, saying, 'Master, have patience with me, and I will pay you all.' Then the master of that servant *was moved with compassion*, released him, and forgave him the debt" (vv. 26–27).

When the Bible says he "fell down," the original language includes the thought that he fell upon his knees and touched the ground with his forehead in an act of profound humility. The verb indicates that he didn't do this once, but over and over again, showing complete surrender. This touched the master's heart.

When Jesus stated that the master "was moved with compassion," He used the passive voice. This means his compassion was released by another's action.

On those occasions where a person who wounded you comes back with humble and genuine repentance, you likely will be moved by compassion.

But this doesn't usually happen. Most people never apologize to us. Recognizing that, the second type of compassion is when you open your heart *yourself*. The second verse outlines the typical experience where you must open your own heart in order to forgive.

Should you not also have had compassion *on your fellow servant, just as I had pity on you? (v. 33, emphasis added)*

In contrast to the previous verse, "should you not also have had compassion" is in the active, not the passive voice. This conveys that the responsibility for action lies with us. It is not dependent on another. We do the act of extending compassion regardless, sometimes in spite of the other person's unrepentance.

Jesus then went one step further, stating "just as I had pity [compassion] on you."

These simple words capture a greater truth. Since God forgave us a far greater debt, should not we forgive those who have sinned against us to a far lesser degree? This is what God requires of all of us.

When we fail to show compassion to a person who has deeply wounded or injured us, we devalue their humanity, feeling that they are unworthy of our forgiveness. One powerful method to release our compassion is to recognize that we have no idea what was going on in the life of the person when they wounded us. Though it does not minimize the depth or wrongness of their crime to consider, perhaps they themselves were carrying deep wounds. Perhaps they were suffering deeply when they hurt us.

Perhaps the person who wounded us was experiencing:

- Grief over news that their fifteen-year-old daughter is pregnant
- Emotional turmoil as a result of new medication
- Fear of the future after losing their job
- Trauma after accidentally running over the neighbor's dog

Think about the person who hurt you the most. Can you give them a gift they do not deserve? Can you extend the compassion of Jesus as one human being to another? Can you release kindness to them even when, *especially* when, it is not deserved?

Extending compassion to another person in no way excuses or minimizes what they did to you. No matter what was going on in a person's life at the time, they still are fully accountable for their actions. But, in order to extend them compassion, set that aside for a moment and see them as a person. What they did is not equal to who they are. When you give them compassion, you focus on them as a person, not on what they did to you.

After all, don't you long for that compassion yourself?

Requirement 3: Release the person from your heart-prison.

Then the master of that servant was moved with compassion, released him, and forgave him the debt. (v. 27)

We would expect that the next thing the master did after being moved with compassion was to simply forgive the servant, but he didn't. Instead nestled between "compassion" and "forgive" are the unexpected words "released him."

In order to release someone, they must be bound. In the case of this story, the "wicked servant" (v. 32) would soon be in prison for his debt. But as the parable isn't really presenting an actual case but the underlying issue of forgiveness, I believe the issue of "releasing" the person from our heart-prison is one of the great missing protocols of God's full forgiveness.

In order to make this step more practical for you, imagine your heart with a door on the top. Open the door and you'll see the steps leading down to the dungeon below with locked cells on both sides of the hallway. Whenever we choose not to forgive a person, we secretly move them into one of our cells, lock the door, turn our backs, and walk away.

All of us have experienced the result of having been locked in another person's heart-prison. Whenever our children become rebellious against us, they have unforgiveness toward us due to a wound we committed against them, even if we don't have any idea what we did. Often we'll feel as though we cannot seem to connect or "get through" to our children. Why? They locked us in their heart-prison and threw away the key.

85

This happens in every single marriage that is nearing divorce.

We have to choose to let go of the people who have wounded us. We do this by a conscious effort to no longer hold on to our desire to imprison them. We'll help you down those stairs in the next chapter. Any idea of who you have locked away in your heart-prison? If you are like most of us, your prison holds more than one unforgiven person.

In like manner, when anyone places their full trust in the death and resurrection of Jesus as payment for their debt of sin, God sets them free (releases them) from the kingdom of darkness and transfers them into the kingdom of Jesus Christ.

He has delivered [to transfer from one place to another] us from the power of darkness and conveyed us into the kingdom of the Son of His love, in whom we have redemption through His blood, the forgiveness of sins. (Col. 1:13–14)

What is unexpected is that the master releases the person *before* he forgives him: "was moved with compassion, *released him*, and forgave him the debt." The order may be far more important than it may appear.

When you have compassion (step 2), you have compassion on the *person*, not on the sin they committed. It's because of your compassion on the person that you can release them from your heart-prison. This is truly unconditional love, isn't it? To release them *before* you forgive them.

There is deep truth working here. This requires something you may never have done before: to separate the person (release them) from the specific wounds that he or she may have committed.

Think of it this way. The person is not equal in any way to the painful act that they committed against you. That was an act they committed and only equates to a short length of time in their lifetime. It doesn't take into consideration that they are a human person like you, who at times does things that you shouldn't as well. Great victory follows as you separate the person from their trespass. Tragically, we magnify the importance of the wound and decrease the importance of the person.

> To prepare for the next chapter, write on your private notes: "I'm going to release (name of person who wounded you), knowing that they are separate from the wounds that they have caused me. They have been in my heart-prison long enough!"

To do this, you must make a separation from the individual and the wound they gave you. The person isn't equal to what they did to you. The wound was an act they did. You could have been best friends for twenty years before they wounded you, but because of that one action you put them in prison. To release them, you are extending compassion on the person, not on what they did to you! Because you have compassion you can choose to let them out of the prison. You will walk through this in the next chapter. But know this now—you are the only one with the key to that prison door.

No one can release them but you.

Requirement 4: Forgive the person for each trespass, offense, mistake, and wound.

Then the master of that servant was moved with compassion, released him, and forgave him the debt. *(Matt. 18:27)*

You have opened your heart, extended compassion, and released them from your heart-prison. You are now ready to forgive them for the specific wounds they did to you.

As you do, the infection in your heart drains.

Matthew 18:35 reveals how we are to do this important step:

"So My heavenly Father also will do to you if each of you, from his heart, does not *forgive his brother his trespasses*." Did you see it? Jesus didn't say to forgive the *person*, nor did He say to "forgive the *trespass*." Instead, He opens our eyes to recognize the heavenly protocol—we must forgive each one of the "*trespasses*."

That has been the unseen root of so many of our problems— we say "I forgive you," instead of "I forgive you for the wound when you _____ (describe the wound)." Honesty and specificity is needed—looking at and naming each and every offense and then forgiving them one at a time. Leaving nothing out. Each wound is a different source of heart infection and unforgiveness. This is often why any previous attempts at forgiveness haven't worked permanently. Though we may have meant the forgiveness we extended, we didn't take the time to remove *all the infection*, consciously forgiving each and every wound.

Christ's use of the plural, *trespasses*, cannot be missed. Our unforgiveness will not be fully completed until we choose to forgive each and every wound the person did. That means you must make a list of all the specific wounds that they inflicted.

Please don't try to forgive without listing and then forgiving each and every wound. If you think you can avoid this step, you are breaking God's protocol and the forgiveness will unfortunately not be complete. Incomplete forgiveness is still unforgiveness and the legal contract will not be annulled. You must release the person separately from forgiving the wounds. The first half is who you release, and the second half is what you forgive.

Now, let's return to our mental picture to complete this crucial step on a practical level. By this time, you have set them free from your heart-prison and you and the now-freed prisoner are standing outside in the bright sunlight. You have released them as a person, and it's finally time to learn how to forgive them for every one of their wounding actions.

Now picture yourself standing outside in the glorious sunshine with that person who used to be locked in your heart-prison. Off to the side in a small box is stacked a pile of jagged rocks, each representing a specific wound this person did to you.

You can see it clearly now, can't you? Though they committed them, they aren't the wounds. Visualize taking that person and walking twenty-five steps away from the rocks. Turn and point to the pile and picture yourself saying, "From my heart, I forgive you for each and every wound that you did those many days ago.

Prepare yourself for the next chapter in which you will forgive each and every wound, one at a time. Each time you forgive another wound your heart heals again and one of those rocks disintegrates until all that remains is an empty box. Take out a piece of paper, and under the name of the person who wounded you the most, list each wound you can remember. When you cannot think of any more, ask God to bring to your memory any you may have forgotten.

Requirement 5: Bless and do good to the person.

But I say to you, love your enemies, bless those who curse you, do good to those who hate you, and pray for those who spitefully use you and persecute you, that you may be sons of your Father in heaven; for He makes His sun rise on the evil and on the good, and sends rain on the just and on the unjust. (Matt. 5:44–45)

This isn't in the Matthew 18 parable, but from the overall teaching of the Bible, it is the final step, like stitching a wound and covering it with healing ointment. Whenever unforgiveness has existed for a long time, you have slid down that Slide of Unforgiveness. Your desire for justice has turned to a desire for vengeance. You wish the person harm. They have become an enemy—and therefore this verse applies.

Look carefully at those four commands Christ outlines for anyone who brings us pain: love, bless, do good, and pray for them. After extending compassion on the person, releasing them from your heart-prison, and forgiving them of all their trespasses, your heart is finally free to obey those commands.

In fact, your freedom to bless the very person who wounded you is also useful as proof-positive confirmation that forgiveness is finally *complete*. How will you *know* if you have truly forgiven? If you can look right at that person who hurt you so much, and *bless them*. You will know that you are free when you can wish well the one who wounded you. You are *free*.

Although blessing the "wounder" in your life may seem impossible at this point, you have only learned the five steps, and not until the next chapter will you actually experience each step. In preparation for your act of forgiveness, picture the one person you may feel as though you never could bless. That is the first person you are going to forgive, and I can promise you, after releasing and forgiving them, you are going to experience the miracle of blessing them with all of your heart!

After leading many people through the first four steps, I have watched person after person reach step five and find themselves genuinely surprised that they are able to bless people who only moments before they could not think of without anger and even revulsion. Often tears stream during this loving act—you now care deeply for another person, often a person who is broken, perhaps far from God as we all once were.

It's at this point that God begins to pour peace into your life. The parable has been lived, the debt forgiven. You look like your King.

Your face will soften; tenderness will come into your voice.

When we bless the one who has been our enemy, it is a love that should feel familiar.

It's the love that Jesus has for each one of us.

CHAPTER EIGHT

Forgiving Others

ENDING THE SUFFERING
BROUGHT BY OTHER PEOPLE

"Forgive others, not because they deserve forgiveness,
but because you deserve peace."

—ANONYMOUS

Congratulations on getting to this point!
You have learned the hidden connection between unforgiveness and torment and prepared your heart to open in true forgiveness.

Freedom is so close. It's time to move into action, taking the steps that will finally release those who have wounded you, release you from the bondage of unforgiveness, and release God's power in your life.

Two forces have drawn you to this point. The first is God, your heavenly Father, who deeply desires that you forgive so that as your character imitates His, His discipline toward you can cease. As it is with any loving parent who disciplines a wayward child,

God's heart is as grieved as yours at your pain. He never desires that His children live outside His peace.

The second force? Your own heart and soul. Now that you see the true links between unforgiveness and resultant pain, you want to run in the other direction—toward freedom, peace, and love. Toward forgiveness.

In this chapter, you're going to walk through three stages. The first will prepare you to forgive. The second will lead you specifically through the five requirements as you forgive others. The final stage focuses on how to enjoy complete forgiveness from God and His cancelation of all torment.

Follow the prompts on these pages, doing *exactly* what is indicated for each step. It is not enough to just read and think. It is not enough to just flip through and consider. You must not dismiss any step as unimportant or unnecessary. The five steps Jesus revealed must be followed in order to receive complete forgiveness and freedom. This must be done right, once and for all.

How I wish we could sit together and have a cup of coffee as we move through each step. Please trust me as we move forward. If you do, I can promise you will succeed; you'll experience exhilarating joy and freedom. Relax. Don't allow any stress or fear to trouble your heart. You are at the very place God wants you to be.

It is time.

These next pages represent the most important section of the entire book, because you are going to help write them. They will become part of your life story. It's finally time to open your heart, extend compassion, release everyone locked inside your heart-prison, forgive all their trespasses, and bless them.

Here's what you'll need for these next steps:

- this book (check!)
- the private notes you've made while reading this book
- several fresh pages of paper

As you prepare, eliminate distractions. Turn off your phone (yes, really). Close your computer. Go to a quiet place, as peaceful as you can find. Let family know that you're not to be disturbed for a while. Get tea, coffee, or water, and relax.

STAGE #1: PREPARING TO FORGIVE

Before you can even begin the first step, you must choose to commit that you will forgive everyone for everything. By solidifying that foundational decision, you will no longer be stuck in indecision or double-mindedness. Leave all procrastination behind.

> Among the tools of life-change is when we state our commitment out loud. Please read this as an expression of your commitment. As you read, allow your mind, will, and heart to come into complete agreement:
>
> *"I have decided of my own free will to forgive everyone who has ever wounded me—intentionally or accidentally. I will fulfill the five requirements Jesus outlined so all my heart infection and torment will completely end. I will not postpone or allow anything to hinder my victory—I will forgive today. Right now!"*

It's vital to not just think these as thoughts, but to use our voices to state our important conviction. You'll experience more peace as you do.

> Now, identify the people in your life whom you need to forgive. Anticipate a little emotional pushback, but overcome it; after all, you've been avoiding this for some time.

Don't let a little bit of anxiety stop you! Now, please pray this simple prayer out loud for God's guidance—it pleases Him because He will notice your humility:

"Dear God, I am committed to forgive everyone who I have not forgiven. Would You please bring to my memory everyone from my life that You know I need to forgive? I trust You to guide and strengthen me."

Now take out your paper and list the names of the people who come to your mind from that prayer. Years ago, when I first listed all the people who wounded me, it filled most of a page. Don't hurry the process. When you are done with your list, ask God one more time, "Lord, have I missed anyone? Please lead me." Expect a couple of other names. You'll have inner peace when your list is complete.

Since unforgiveness is directly against God and not just other people, you will want to know the people on His list—that's why you just asked for His help and guidance. Do not hurry this or only think there's only one or two people—you may have many. The first time I made my list, I surely did and it went all the way back to my childhood.

Now take that list of names that God prompted you to consider, and rank them in order—from the most difficult to forgive to the easiest. Always start with the hardest, who you wrote down as number one.

Now turn that sheet of paper over. At the top, write

down the number one person's name and then begin listing every single wound that they were a part of—whether or not they intended to wound you. Wounds occur whether the person intended it or didn't (such as an automobile accident). You may only have a few wounds, but some people have dozens of unforgiven wounds that have accumulated over the years from particular individuals. The ship's doctor had two and a half pages of wounds.

Now, look over the list and number the three most difficult wounds from one to three. You already anticipate that you will forgive first the most difficult wound from the most difficult person to forgive. When that happens in the next few moments, you'll be able to forgive the rest of the list far more easily than you can yet imagine.

Before we move to the first step of the process, state the name of the number one person out loud: _____ (name). Then state: "In the next few moments, I will forgive _____ (name) for every wound they ever committed, including the wound of _____ (the hardest one)." Engage your will, no matter how it feels. Say that sentence out loud. As you do, you are gaining ground that you have lost.

STAGE #2: THE FIVE STEPS TO FORGIVE

Here we are. It's time to forgive.

As we move through these steps, be sure to saturate each one in prayer, continually reminding yourself to keep an open heart and extend compassion toward

those who have wronged you. Pursue your full freedom. You are so close!

Step 1: Open your heart.

You're about to forgive the person who wounded you the most. Just the thought of opening your heart can raise anxiety for a moment or two. That's normal. Will you allow me to guide you to an open heart? Move forward through it. Slowly repeat the following state-ments out loud:

- "I am committed to forgive right now. I shall achieve forgiveness because God has given me His power to forgive. I recognize that I should have done this much earlier, but today is a new day in my life."

- "I choose to overcome my hesitations and contrary emotions, to follow the requirements for true forgive-ness that Jesus Christ revealed. I will not allow anyone or anything to hinder me from this—what I have cho-sen of my own free will to do."

- "I release my heart from the inner bondage of a blocked and closed heart. I tear down the walls that have kept others out and locked me in—a captive for far too long. I open my heart and stop protecting it from the tem-porary discomfort that I may experience as I begin to forgive these old wounds."

If any of those sentences were difficult to speak out loud, read them again, still out loud but more slowly, until you truly feel that your heart is opening to this process. If this brings up any difficult memories, please take all the time you need to process, because on the other side of forgiveness, these wounds are healed, and all that remains is a scar.

Step 2: Extend compassion.

Compassion moves our heart toward forgiveness. Thankfully, releasing our compassion doesn't need to be difficult. As we've seen before, we need to separate wounds inflicted upon us from the people who made them.

There is never, *ever* a valid excuse for someone's sin, abuse, trauma, or wounds toward us. But there are often factors in another's life that help us humanize and understand them better. We have no idea what another person has suffered, including the ones who have hurt us. We don't know what they were going through at the time they hurt us.

Whatever the severity of their action, we need to see them as a human being. To do that requires you to be a bigger person. You must take these first steps, even if you struggle a bit during the process. Isn't that the way of the cross? "Not My will, but Yours, be done," Jesus said to the Father (Luke 22:42). It does not mean that you brush over their hurtful actions. It means that you face them head-on, choosing to see the person behind it, and *granting them the gift of your compassion.*

Take a moment and write a couple of compassionate sentences on your sheet about your number one person who wounded you. Remember—the goal is to separate them from their action and choose to grant them your compassion and grace. Here are a few suggestions of things to write:

- "I couldn't know what was going on in _____'s (name) life at the time."
- "I don't know if _____ (name) was struggling with depression, rejection, abuse, or something else that may have attributed to his or her action against me."

- "I extend my compassion to _____ (name) as a person as I also have hurt others."
- Add your own, tailored to each situation. Remember—be honest, in no way minimizing your wound, but choose to grant the gift of your compassion.

If you are struggling with thinking or writing some understanding sentences, your heart may not be used to extending grace and mercy to others. That's okay; now is a great time to begin. When we grant another person mercy, our condemning attitude ceases. When we grant another person grace, we give them kindness and tenderness as an undeserved gift. They may not deserve it, but we need to give it!

Whenever anyone struggles to complete this stage of forgiveness, I ask them if they have ever hurt other people. Sometimes I ask them to share a couple of stories from their own life. As they do, their heart makes the all-important connection: *We all wound others, and I'm no exception.* The severity and impact of our wounding actions and attitudes may vary widely, but the root reality is there. We all hurt other people. We all need forgiveness.

"How have I wounded someone?" Ask yourself that question. Don't allow it to become a source of shame or guilt, but allow that memory to soften your heart toward the person who wounded you. We all need forgiveness. We all need compassion. So does the person who is awaiting your compassion.

If you have successfully completed this step, your heart has not only opened, but you have a new-found tenderness and understanding toward your number one wounder, _____ (name).

Quiet your heart. Do you feel more open toward that person? If you don't, gently go deeper into your heart until you can give them your compassion.

> When you are ready, state:
>
> *I have opened my heart to _____ (name) and extended my compassion to them. I no longer condemn them for what they did but grant them my mercy, compassion, and kindness in spite of how they hurt me.*

Step 3: Release the person from your inner heart-prison.

Your imagination is a wonderful gift from God, and it's time to use that gift to help you forgive. Recall the picture of the door in your heart, the stairs, and the cells on both sides of the aisle. Now with your imagination use that picture to help you release your number one person from the cell they have been locked in for so long. Imagine this happening step by step:

Because your heart now is compassionate, walk over and open the door on your heart. You walk through it. As you make your way down the stairwell, you hear sounds of misery in the distance. You make your way down the darkened hallway until you see the person who hurt you the most standing inside a cell of prison bars. You quietly walk over to their cell. You look at their face, then miraculously express your compassion and kindness to them. Watch their face.

You reach into your pocket and take out a rusty key. You unlock their prison door. "I'm sorry for locking you here for so long," you say. "I release you. You are free!" You fling open the door.

Allow yourself to feel the release as they run out of the cell and embrace you. Finally, picture them weeping with regret for what they did, and rejoicing because you finally let them out—Hallelujah! Together, walk up those stairs into the bright light of forgiveness and freedom.

Now that you have released this person who has hurt you, the next step is to forgive them for each wound you have experienced, whether or not they were even aware of them.

Step 4: Forgive the person for each wound.

As you work through this step, keep Christ's words in mind, "forgive his brother his trespasses." Christ's language assumes there will be more than one trespass. Although that's not always the case, it often is. Why? Because a major wound nearly always is accompanied by other wounds that occurred as a result of it.

I remember working through this with a woman who had grown up with an alcoholic mother. The more she and I talked about her wounds, the more she began to see *other* wounds connected to the main one. She wept as she described what her mother's alcoholism did to her younger brother and sister. How she was so embarrassed when her friends came over and found her mother drunk on the sofa—who started yelling at all of them. She never invited her friends to her house ever again. Her list on her sheet grew as she reviewed dozens of wounds over the years. Each of those wounds were still separately infected. They were all connected, like the links of a thick chain, but she had lost something different with each one.

Lean into this reality with courage. Acknowledge your hurt and loss honestly. To push them out of your mind is not to live in reality. All your wounds are real, but they are in the past—even the ones whose consequences you still live with. It's okay. It's over.

But what's *not* over is your healing and freedom through your godly response—forgiving each and every one of those wounds. Your heart will heal a little every time you forgive another wound. And, as I mentioned earlier, once you start forgiving it will become easier and easier. Isn't that good news?

Ready? Let's continue. The person who hurt you the most has now received your heartfelt compassion and has been released from the hidden dungeon in your heart. Now it's time to forgive each wounding experience that they caused:

> Take another look at the back of your paper with the name of the person who wounded you the most and the list of all the wounds you wrote down. As you have been reading the last few paragraphs, you probably started remembering other wounds that you had lost track of. Add them to the list—and don't hurry. Let your heart help you make the list. When you cannot remember any more, just check with the Lord for His approval with these words: "Lord, please bring to my mind every single wound that _____ (name) committed that I haven't forgiven." Then wait for about a minute, and you'll probably discover a few more. Don't hurry.

Now you are ready to read out loud the following statements and fill in the wounder's name as you go. You've already completed the first three steps of forgiveness—you'll definitely hear it in your voice when you start forgiving with your heart. Forgiveness moves from something in your mind, to your will, and finally to your heart. Give yourself some grace to forgive from your heart. Read these statements out loud and slowly. The further down the list you read, the more you should focus on speaking from your heart. You're almost there!

- "I've committed right now to forgive _____ (name) for each and every wound."

- "I've had unforgiveness toward them for too long and that is ending right now."

- "I have opened my heart and released _____ (name) from prison, and now I'm going to give _____ (name) a wonderful gift of my complete forgiveness."

- "I forgive _____ (name) for the wound of _____ (name the hardest wound to forgive)."

- "From my heart, I genuinely forgive _____ (name) for the wound of _____ (the same wound)."

- *Slowly now*—"With all of my heart, I fully and completely forgive _____ (name) for the wound of _____ (the same).

- "I fully release _____ (name) for doing _____ (describe the wound) and no longer hold it against them."

By this time, you will sense that *you are actually forgiving them*. If not, you are close. If you need a little more help, read through that same list one more time, putting your hand on your heart and repeating each sentence from your heart.

Now go through the same process with the second hardest wound you must forgive. At this point, with the hardest behind you, you will be able to forgive all the other wounds on the list. You are moving forward so well. Just use this sentence and fill in the next wound, then the next one, and so on. By the third wound you forgive, God will empower you and you will find great freedom to forgive easier and easier. But, God waits for you to take the initial steps—He requires that you choose to forgive—He will not forgive for you.

"From my heart, I genuinely forgive _____ (name) for
the wound of _____ (describe the wound)."

When you are finished with the whole list, you may be wondering if you remembered them all. Thankfully we've developed
a simple tool I call "The Forgiveness Validator." The Forgiveness
Validator gives the Holy Spirit an opportunity to make sure that
everything has been forgiven to His satisfaction.

To validate your forgiveness, make the following declaration
out loud to the Lord from your heart:

"Before God, I have forgiven _____ (name) for every
wound."

Once you make that declaration, be still. Wait. Sit before God.
Usually the Lord will reveal at least one area you missed. Forgive
that, then state the same sentence again. If after a few seconds
your heart remains at peace, you are finished. By stating to God, "I
have forgiven _____ (name) for everything" you have given the
Lord the opportunity to show you if it's true or not. If you have no
further revelations and have a sense of peace, you know for sure
you are finished!

Your unforgiveness toward that person is gone.

Congratulations! Well done.

Now the easiest step is all that is left.

Step 5: Bless and seek ways to do good to them.

This cements the process and gives you confidence that you have
truly forgiven. You cannot truly do this if unforgiveness lingers.
When you bless a person who wounded you, you are fulfilling your
highest calling by responding the same way Jesus did when He was
severely, unfairly, and repeatedly wounded. You are fulfilling His
command in Matthew 5:44–45:

But I say to you, love your enemies, bless those who curse you, do good to those who hate you, and pray for those who spitefully use you and persecute you, that you may be sons of your Father in heaven; for He makes His sun rise on the evil and on the good, and sends rain on the just and on the unjust.

When you have opened your heart, extended compassion, released the person(s) from your heart-prison, and forgiven them of all their trespasses against you, your heart will be fully set free to bless them and wish them well.

Here is the blessing prayer that I pray for those who have wounded me—now it's your turn:

Dear God, I ask You to bless _____ in every way, including their health, spiritual life, marriage, family, business, finances, ministry, and friendships. I ask that You would pour out a greater amount of Your kindness upon _____ because of my prayer for them.

Friend, the reason you can bless and do good to the person you have forgiven is because *you are free indeed!* Prior to forgiving, could you have completed this step? Not hardly. Now you can, and you did. Through God's power, you have broken through into freedom, joy, and peace.

So what about the list of all the other people you need to forgive on the front side of that paper? Go through the same steps. Under each person's name, list the specific wounds and then state out loud the same sentences. You already know your heart is fully free and you actually are drawn to complete the process with everyone!

When you are finished with everyone on your list and all their trespasses against you, use The Forgiveness Validator by stating out loud the following:

"Before God, I have forgiven everyone of everything."

Again, don't hurry this final little section, as you have come so far in such a short amount of time. Normally, the Lord reveals two or three other people. I remember the first time I did this, I had to forgive a grade school teacher! When you finally have peace, it's time to celebrate!

STAGE #3: BEFORE THE LORD

Now that you have forgiven, it's time to ask God to forgive you. Unforgiveness is a sin, and ultimately every sin that is committed by us or anyone else is against God. God, however, is ready and willing to forgive us the moment we ask Him—as that is His protocol for us to receive His forgiveness for our sins. The Bible is straightforward and reveals that unforgiveness, extended anger, bitterness, slander, resentment, hatred, and vengeance are all sins. You have forgiven those who wounded you, and now it's time to experience God's forgiveness as you have wounded His heart.

First John 1:9 says that if we confess our sins to God, He will forgive and cleanse us. So let's ask God for His wonderful forgiveness because of our sin of unforgiveness. You can simply confess to Him by praying,

"Dear God, I confess to You my sins of unforgiveness, anger, bitterness, slander, resentment, hatred, and vengeance. Please forgive me and cleanse me from all unrighteousness. Because I have forgiven everyone of everything, thank You for canceling all torment caused by my unforgiveness. In Jesus' name, Amen."

Once you have confessed your sin of unforgiveness, then ask God to bless your life abundantly. He has eagerly been waiting to do so . . . so *ask!*

When you have finished the process of forgiving everyone and everything on your list and have confessed your sins to God, He responds not only with His forgiveness but also by sovereignly and instantly canceling all legal contracts connected with being delivered to the tormentors.

Many of you have lived decades under the presence of torment and will finally be able to live lighthearted and joyful, without the cloud of pain and darkness that followed you for so long. Such freedom affects every area of life and relationship. We were unaware that at least some of our suffering was connected to our unforgiveness. What a joy you will soon experience, now that you have opened your heart, joining your kind Father in the life of forgiveness and freedom.

You will only begin to realize the significance of what happened today in the days and years ahead.

"Today I opened my heart, extended compassion, released the people from my heart-prison, forgave all their wounds, and blessed them!"

Signature: _____

Date: _____

CHAPTER NINE

Forgiving Yourself: Part One

PREPARING YOUR HEART FOR WHAT'S AHEAD

> "To forgive is to set a prisoner free and discover that the prisoner was you."
>
> —LEWIS B. SMEDES

You have come a long way on this journey. But for most of us, forgiveness is something we need to receive, not just give. And that starts with forgiving ourselves.

Many years ago when I discovered Jesus' revelation about the consequences of unforgiveness, I made my list of all the people who had wounded me. As I prayed and asked God to reveal all those wounds, I was shocked as I remembered hurts from all the way back when I was in the sixth grade with my first "girlfriend," and then scattered throughout my decades of life.

But when I moved into the arena of forgiving myself? I discovered a completely different set of wounds. Deep ones that had affected my life in ways I had never put together. To be honest, some of the oldest ones were the hardest to forgive myself for. Why? They were rooted so deeply after years of neglect.

What husband or wife hasn't wounded their spouse? What parent hasn't wounded their children? Which of us hasn't hurt the people we work alongside, the people we live with, the people who worship with us?

As I reflected over my life the first time I forgave myself, I had to deal with some damaging decisions and actions I had made that hurt other people and myself. Financial missteps. Errors in leadership. Lack of sensitivity to family members. Ah, how painful to forgive oneself when *we* are the source of the hurts of others, especially those we love deeply. But, such freedom when I opened my heart to myself, granted myself much-needed compassion, walked down those heart-prison steps and released myself, forgave myself for my sins and mistakes, and asked God to bless me with freedom I had not known before.

I went back to some of those people I had wounded to ask for their forgiveness. What healing took place!

In fact, just during the third edit of this book, I was surprised to find myself recalling a wound I had caused in another person that I realized had never been resolved. My heart grieved for a couple of days as I wrote a heart-felt letter to them. I asked my precious wife to read the letter, and she suggested a few more tender words to add. Sometimes we need to allow others to speak into our process of forgiveness, to point out things that we might not see. Something broke free in my heart when I finally put that envelope in the mailbox. Then I sat down and forgave myself for that hurtful action of long ago.

I cannot even begin to tell you how dramatically my life changed when I forgave others and myself. Thank God for His revelation and the freedom resulting in obedience to His divine protocols. Maybe it's your time to break free as well.

There are as many ways that we wound ourselves as there are ways to wound others. But we often don't think in terms of looking in the mirror and releasing *ourselves* from our heart-prison, letting God cleanse the wounds we've inflicted on our own hearts. So what prevents us from forgiving ourselves? And what happens if we don't?

Let me tell another story as we consider those questions.

After one speaking engagement, I was approached by a businessman who was visibly distressed. He invited me to a nearby café. As we ate lunch, he told me his story.

He was a wealthy man. He loved God and his work. He explained that he had the gift of generosity, and he and his wife had been saving up in order to give God a massive amount of money. In a special secret account, he had managed over the course of his life to save $26 million, all earmarked to be given away to God's work when the time was right. In order to multiply the money, he made the decision to invest it all in an exciting tech startup company.

He had done his homework, all the necessary due diligence and research such a tremendous investment demanded, and the math worked out. He was confident the investment would grow at least four times. Unfortunately, that is not what happened. What he didn't foresee was the drastic downturn that would unexpectedly sweep the market. The company he invested in went bankrupt and he lost the $26 million. He now felt like a total failure because he had lost it all—every single cent! He said to me, "I have no reason to live, God must be furious with me, and I have ruined my life. I've sinned greatly against the Lord."

"But how did you sin?" I asked. "Where in the Bible does it say that losing a carefully researched investment is a sin?" The light began to dawn as he considered the fact that a human mistake is not the same as a sin against God.

"What was your motive for saving and investing the money?" I asked.

"I wanted to give more money to God's kingdom," he replied.

"Do you think that your heart pleased God?" I asked. He slowly nodded as the light started dawning. I continued: "If God knew you were going to give that gift to Him, don't you believe He had the ability to keep you from losing that money if He chose?"

"Sure," he said, "God is sovereign. He knows all things."

"Now, can you forgive yourself for making a mistake?" I asked. "Even though it was a lot of money, it's only money. God is more concerned about your heart than He is your cash." The words connected. Amid tears, he forgave himself and left our table a lighter man. A free man. A rejoicing man. You see, both our sins and mistakes can wound our hearts.

But not all stories end this way.

Self-deception is a terrible tragedy. But God's power can cut through any shame or guilt, to help us see clearly, acknowledge our sin or mistake, and move to a place of healing. As you continue through this chapter, pray that God would open your eyes and help your heart to be at peace as you prepare to forgive yourself.

One day I received a call from another man I didn't know. To be honest, I'm not even sure how he got my number. Like the man in the previous story, he was in financial crisis. His voice was beyond anxious. He spoke fast and loud. He sounded as if he was in serious trouble. No sooner than I said, "This is Bruce," I could almost feel his torment through the phone, shouting. "I blew it, I blew it!"

He was halfway into his story before I even got his name.

He also had made some unwise financial investments. For some reason he was emotionally persuaded that the Lord was leading him to take financial risks that he normally wouldn't have. In fact, he told me he felt an inner compulsion to invest in a way that went against the expertise and wisdom he had gained from his life in finance. When all the chips settled, his money was gone. All of it. His business and family both were bankrupted.

I tried to talk to him, to get a word in, but no matter what I said, he remained inconsolable. He would not face reality—that as bad as this felt, it wasn't the end of the world. He wouldn't listen as I begged him to forgive himself and begin again—as so many have before him.

My words were not being received. I could hear the struggle; his voice was hardening, becoming stubborn in his fixation on his mistake. He finally said, "I've ruined my life—the life of my entire family. I know God can forgive me, but I can't forgive myself."

And the last words I heard were the words that began our conversation— "I blew it, I *blew* it."

The next day he took his own life.

Both of these men struggled to forgive themselves. They wrestled intensely with the torment of self-hatred and self-vengeance they held over themselves. They didn't need to forgive someone else; but they desperately needed to forgive *themselves*. Whether or not they had sinned or made a major mistake, their lives were being ruined by the debt they held against themselves, a debt they felt could never be repaid.

Millions of people struggle to forgive themselves as these two men did. In fact, I've learned that at least 30 percent of people when asked, "Who wounded you the deepest?" answer, "It's *me*." They often follow that by saying, "And I'll never forgive myself."

Their issue may not have anything at all to do with money. It can be anything. Perhaps their inner war stems from committing adultery that resulted in a painful divorce, or an addiction to alcohol or drugs that eventually resulted in their losing job after job, or an abortion with all the tragic lifelong consequences, or dropping out of school and being trapped in a dead-end job, or breaking the law and going to prison. Regardless what the self-inflicted wound may be, whether sin or merely a mistake, they are unable to set themselves free. They are unable to look in the mirror and say, "I forgive you."

Until now.

WHY WE DON'T FORGIVE OURSELVES

Are you haunted by a past sin or mistake? Are you unable to stop thinking about it, feeling depressed every time those obsessive thoughts cross your mind? You would do anything to be able to go back and undo it.

If so, you haven't forgiven yourself. And you *need* to.

First, a heads-up: this chapter isn't about those things we do for which we naturally forgive ourselves. Oftentimes there are things for which we naturally forgive ourselves that don't bother us and never surface again in our hearts. We feel the infraction is just *life*, one of those things that happens and it is okay with us. Do you realize that what you are really saying is, "Whatever happened, my heart didn't become wounded"? Therefore, you find no reason to forgive yourself.

Instead, this chapter focuses on major wounds that caused a deeper level of trauma to us or someone else. I've yet to meet anyone anywhere in the world who has not wounded themselves or others in a deep way—we all have. But it's the rare person, though, who thinks deeply enough to recognize that unforgiveness toward yourself has just as many negative results in your life as when another person wounds you. Sometimes more.

> Consider the following list and try to imagine the wounds that occurred when any of these actions occurred at some time in our life whether in the past or present—because they all can result in deep wounds in a person's life:

- Alcoholism
- Divorce
- Use of narcotics
- Financial mistake that cost you a great deal of money—even your house
- Bankruptcy and the suffering that follows
- Violent act such as hitting or wounding with a knife or gun
- Major violation of the law and prison time
- Addiction to pornography
- Lied to or cheated someone with great resulting harm
- Abortion or pressuring another to have an abortion
- Car or motorcycle accident that maimed you or someone else
- Molestation or other serious sexual misconduct
- Hurting our children through neglect, abandonment, or abuse
- Let God down in a major way that you still regret
- Adultery
- Failure in business where your dream died

- Broken ministry
- Incest
- Racial violence or acts of prejudice
- Abusive behavior toward someone (physical, verbal, or emotional)
- Rape
- Abandoning someone who was depending on us

Very few of us can read this list without identifying with one or more. Unfortunately, the sin nature is still very much alive in the human race.

The point of this chapter is not about if you did any of these things, but rather, will you choose to forgive yourself for what you did—and accept God's forgiveness as well? If you became addicted to a certain damaging habit that you did repeatedly, just imagine the size and number of resulting wounds.

Just as there are lies that hold us back for forgiving others, so there are lies that keep us from forgiving ourselves. They're like prison guards barring your door to freedom from torment, from the freedom your heart was made for.

As we progress into forgiving ourselves, we'll cover some new ground and ideas in addition to those in the previous chapter. There are some vital new concepts necessary to forgiving yourself that need to be brought out. The review will more deeply cement these important steps into your heart for when you need them in the future.

Let's dismiss these lies with the truth. Today, may you rise up and embrace the freedom you so desperately need that comes by *forgiving yourself.*

⁂

Lie: **I don't need to forgive myself.**
Truth: **If you have done wrong to others or yourself, you do need to forgive yourself.**

Too many of us have limited our understanding of the scope of forgiveness. We are taught that we need to forgive others and that we need God to forgive us—but can you ever remember anyone teaching or encouraging you to forgive *yourself*? For many, this thought never seems to crystallize in their thinking. And, because it remains behind a muddled wall, we never seem to pursue it.

Both men in the previous stories didn't need to forgive others; they needed to forgive themselves. One did. He went on with purpose and freedom while the other sank to the depths of despair—and exacted vengeance upon himself by ending his life. While everyone will not go to that extreme, far too many of us are dying a slow death emotionally, relationally, and spiritually due to living daily a life confined in a personal prison of unforgiveness. The suffering brought by our own unforgiveness of self is very real, isn't it?

Lie: **I have to make myself suffer enough—then I can forgive myself.**

Truth: God has already disciplined you if you needed it. Your self-inflicted suffering is useless.

Whenever a person reaches the stage of vengeance in the Slide of Unforgiveness related to themselves, they are locked into a relentless cycle of seeking to atone or pay for their sins or mistakes. But this harsh reality is fruitless. It never ends.

What do I mean "it never ends"? To this date, I have yet to find even one person who decided they had suffered enough to forgive themselves. Not one. Why? Because we become addicted to self-sabotage and punishment.

You can't make yourself suffer enough for what you did. Only one person's suffering is sufficient enough to atone for your sin, and His name is Jesus. Inflicting punishment and vengeance on yourself doesn't change one thing, nor will it help anything. Can you face the reality that all the suffering you consciously and subconsciously lashed on yourself is totally unnecessary and useless? It's empty suffering. Pain in vain.

Sure there may be some painful consequences for your actions. There may be repentance and restitution you need to make. And, often God has disciplined you already, or still is, for those sins that either have not been repented of or discontinued. God doesn't appreciate your help in His discipline.

However, making yourself suffer for your transgressions is not wise, healthy, productive, or necessary. What is necessary is that you embrace the teaching of Jesus and forgive the person who wounded you—yourself.

Lie: **I won't suffer if I don't forgive myself.**
Truth: **All unforgiveness results in personal torment.**

Here is a tragic lie we embrace: "So what if I don't forgive myself? It won't affect my life."

Out of sight, out of mind? That's simply not the truth. Why? Because unforgiveness toward yourself is still unforgiveness, and unforgiveness always has predictable painful consequences due to God delivering you to the torturers until you forgive all your trespasses. If you have anyone, including yourself, locked in your heart-prison, the legal sentence of unforgiveness is in effect. And by being in effect, you will experience the effects of the sentence. You already know what those consequences include from our study of the word *basanizo*—so why endure this unnecessary suffering? End it through forgiveness.

Lie: **What I did happened so long ago there is no need for me to forgive myself.**

Truth: Time does not and cannot heal unforgiveness.

Time doesn't heal all wounds. They need to be cleansed. If a physical wound is infected, time will only worsen it; same with the heart. It worsens because time permits the seeds of unforgiveness to grow and mature as it slides further down into the pit of self-hatred and self-vengeance. If it feels "better," perhaps it is because you are growing numb the deeper the pain goes.

⚜

Lie: **I'm too unworthy. I don't deserve to be forgiven.**
Truth: Forgiveness is for everyone. You are not the first and only exception.

Thoughts and feelings of unworthiness are either from people who treated you as though you were unworthy of respect or from actions or sins you committed that you realized were damaging but did not forgive yourself for. The guilt and shame you have experienced as a result of these actions have subtly convinced you that you indeed are not a good person and therefore unworthy. Feelings of unworthiness are almost always rooted in unforgiveness toward others and ourselves.

Well, may I welcome you to the human race? All of us hurt others, whether we intended to or not. All of us make foolish or naïve decisions that result in great pain to ourselves. All of us sin against God in a whole range of areas—lying, stealing, hatred, immorality, gluttony, selfishness, and more. The list is so very long. Since you know this is true, what makes you think you are beyond redemption—that your unworthy actions and attitudes are so far worse than any of us? Could there be a well-disguised root of pride and arrogance veiled deep in your soul? Did you think you were better than the rest of us—and that you were shocked at your faults and sins? Did you commit adultery like King David and then issue an assassination command for the husband of the woman you slept with? Did you commit incest with your children like Abraham's nephew Lot? Did you deny Jesus Christ after three years of intense one-on-one with Him—not just once, but three times and even swore in the midst of it? I could go on and on, but I think you get the point. Who among us could ever argue with the verse "for all have sinned and fall short of the glory of God" (Rom. 3:23)?

From one unworthy person to another—you have been created in the image of God and are "worthy" of complete forgiveness. That's why God the Father sent His Son Jesus Christ to die for your sins. God views you so worthy that He sent someone to die to redeem you. And since God views you with such high value, why have you decided He's wrong?

Whenever I have helped a person full of these feelings of unworthiness to forgive others and themselves, and receive God's forgiveness—guess what happens? All feelings of unworthiness evaporate. Why? Because the basis of your unworthiness has been erased and forgotten, thrown as far away as the east is from the west. Isn't it a time to embrace this supernatural gift of forgiveness (since forgiveness was established by the Godhead in heaven) for yourself? You are worthy to receive your own gift of mercy and grace. Forgive yourself and leave those damaging feelings behind, for good. You may still feel that you don't deserve it, but you need it and you have the power to give it. So why not grant yourself that merciful gift now!

God is willing to forgive everybody for everything because of the shed blood of Jesus. We don't have to be worthy to be forgiven. If we did, none of us would qualify. Forgiveness is a gift, and a gift is not given because of worthiness. It is given out of love—out of mercy and compassion. So instead of focusing on the terrible things you may have done, focus on extending mercy and compassion to yourself. What a difference that will make.

Lie: I've done the same thing over and over. How can I forgive myself?

Truth: Forgiveness only can be granted for wounds from the past. Your future choices are a different issue.

In Matthew 18:22, how many times did Jesus tell Peter to forgive his brother? Remember—"seventy times seven." In other words, Jesus told him to forgive his brother as often as necessary. You are to forgive yourself the same way—as much as necessary. The fact that you may engage repeatedly in behaviors or attitudes harmful to yourself or others signals that you have an underlying need for help. But that is separate from the act of forgiveness. God wants you to be free—free to forgive yourself and free to live a lifestyle that is pleasing to Him. Perhaps some or all of the anxiety and distress you may be feeling will disappear when you forgive yourself—and take away the inner compulsion to continue any inappropriate habits.

True repentance is needed at this point, thoroughly turning from any pattern of sin, turning toward God and seeking His forgiveness.

To aid in your process of repentance, here is a prayer to use. Pray it from your heart:

Lord, You are holy and righteous. You know all of my sins and failings—what I've done and what I've left undone. Please forgive me for every way I have hurt others, hurt myself, or hurt Your heart. I repent before You from my heart, turning from my sin toward You. Thank You for Your grace and forgiveness. Help me walk in holiness before You. In Jesus' name, Amen.

Now that you understand some of the reasons that may be hindering you from forgiving yourself, let's return to The Slide of Unforgiveness with a focus on how it works when you don't forgive yourself. There is important expansion of the principles beyond forgiving others—so don't miss them. You'll see and understand yourself better as we explore the seven stages.

THE SLIDE OF UNFORGIVENESS OF YOURSELF

Think back to the two businessmen struggling to forgive themselves at the beginning of the chapter. I want to highlight another facet of their story that we can't afford to miss.

We know how the story ended for each of those men. One man forgave and found freedom. The other failed to forgive and ended up taking his own life. While each man had his own "good" reason for not forgiving himself, as long as that unforgiveness persisted, both were changing for the worse. They both were cascading down the same slide of unforgiveness that we discussed in previous chapters. Only this time the cause was not them failing to forgive others, but themselves. This is the tragic way any one of us will change when we don't forgive the person we see in the mirror every day. It's time to return to that slide.

Remember the downward progression:

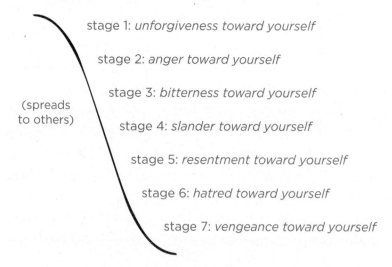

stage 1: *unforgiveness toward yourself*

stage 2: *anger toward yourself*

stage 3: *bitterness toward yourself*

(spreads to others)

stage 4: *slander toward yourself*

stage 5: *resentment toward yourself*

stage 6: *hatred toward yourself*

stage 7: *vengeance toward yourself*

Stage 1: Unforgiveness toward yourself

It's the one thing in your life that you hate to think about. Every time the thought of what happened crosses your mind, you cringe. In your mind forgiving yourself has not been an option. You feel that you can never forgive yourself for what you did—whether it was accidental or intentional. You think the amount of pain and the damaging consequences caused by your actions cannot be undone. You now see not only the act you committed, but yourself as a person who is unforgivable.

Stage 2: Anger toward yourself

How could I be so stupid? you think. *Why in the world would I do such a thing—I thought I was better than that!* These statements are characteristic of a person who is angry at themselves. What happens initially when we fail to forgive ourselves is we try to stuff the memory of what happened, but this only provides momentary relief. Like a dormant volcano, the pressure on the inside builds up, and before you know it, there is an eruption. The anger that has built up on the inside will spill over and affect how you view yourself and how you treat others. To remedy the situation, you may continue to try to stuff the memory, or suffer from increasing and stubborn depression.

Stage 3: Bitterness toward yourself

When we become bitter, the texture of our heart becomes calloused and hard. The necessary qualities we need to love ourselves and have good relationships with others are either no longer present or fading rapidly. We can become untrusting toward others, rebellious, sullen, and withdrawn. You can even find yourself not liking your spouse, your job, your church, your neighbor, and so on. The cynicism that accompanies bitterness discolors everything you see. Also, the internal distress you experience can become so strong that you start to look for various behaviors and people to give you a little comfort. Unfortunately, the comforts that are sought do not help the underlying problem but only mask them for a moment.

Stage 4: Slander against yourself

Have you ever thought to yourself any of these "I am" statements—*"I am not worth it, I am stupid, I am damaged goods,* or *I am a bad person because of the terrible things I have done"*? In this stage, you talk down about yourself with negative self-talk. You make harmful value judgments about yourself as a person—judgments that are not based on God's perception of you, but are the result of not forgiving yourself. The self-slander is something you spread to others too. In your conversations with friends and others, you criticize yourself. With your own mouth you tear yourself down by speaking destructively inwardly and outwardly about yourself as a person. You do this because you feel so bad about yourself that verbally dismantling yourself feels appropriate.

Stage 5: Resentment toward yourself

It's one thing when you resent others, because at least you have the option to stay away from them when you can. But when you resent yourself, where can you go? You can't escape. You keep track of all the "stupid" things that you say and "hurtful" things you do—even innocently. You discover that things that never used to bother you have now become additional reasons for your failures. The lines in your life start to blur and everything becomes justification for your worthlessness and negative condition. In this stage, addictions such as pornography, alcoholism, drug abuse, and illicit sexual activity are rampant. You're searching for any outlet to distance and distract yourself from . . . yourself.

Stage 6: Hatred toward yourself

By the time you have made it to this stage, you are convinced there is nothing worthy about you—you feel inferior, unlovable, and incompetent. You can't stand to be by yourself, and yet you feel unworthy to be with others. There is also an ever-present fear because you believe if people knew what you have done they would never want to be with you. When you are in the throes of self-hatred, you may be tempted to practice destructive behaviors. Often you will find yourself withdrawing, feeling hopeless and powerless to make any changes.

Stage 7: Vengeance toward yourself

You want to make yourself pay for what you've done. You begin to take action to inflict self-punishment. You find yourself unable to cope with success because you feel you need to pay for what you have done. You self-sabotage—getting fired from the job, spending yourself into terrible debt, breaking long-standing friendships. You may hide serious destructive behaviors such as eating disorders, cutting yourself, and suicidal thoughts. You may even attempt suicide to atone for what you have done. You feel that you must make yourself pay for the mistakes you have made.

We've reached the place where everything is now all out in the open. Before us in plain view are the reasons why it's hard for us to forgive ourselves, along with the painful way our life changes when we don't forgive. There is a good chance that you have kept this very private issue close to your chest and have not talked to many people about it. You have suffered in silence and felt so all alone.

Those days are about to be over.

All you have to do is open the door. There are five required steps. Jesus shared them just for you, for where you are at this very moment.

It's beyond time to exit your heart-prison and find the freedom you have always known you were made for.

CHAPTER TEN

Forgiving Yourself: Part Two

ENDING THE SUFFERING WE BRING ON OURSELVES

"For You, Lord, are good, and ready to forgive, and abundant in mercy to all those who call upon You."

—PSALM 86:5

Welcome! You have arrived at the moment of new beginnings. You will soon experience a breakthrough into the freedom, peace, and joy that will be yours when you forgive yourself.

As you did in chapter 8, "Forgiving Others," find a private place where you can relax without any interruptions, including that ever-present cell phone, and sit in God's healing presence. This book deals with some personal and private matters, and you may have had to fight the tendency to procrastinate or avoid the topic. The unrest you may be feeling likely means that this will be an extremely important chapter for you. Let your determination to be set free overcome any hesitation you have at this point.

I have had to return to this place numerous times in my life and will undoubtedly have to again. But, isn't it nice to know you are not alone, that we are in this chapter together, just as we were in chapter 8?

In this chapter, you'll process through three stages of forgiving yourself: preparing to forgive; forgiving through the five requirements; and accepting God's forgiveness.

As you might expect, the five requirements to forgive others and yourself are the same. As you've already experienced the steps to forgiving others, it will be much easier the second time around. Depending on what has happened in your life, this can be either easier or more difficult. For example, if your sin only involves yourself, it may be easier to forgive. If your sin caused deep pain in others' lives, it may be much more difficult. The good news, however, is that this process doesn't take a long time—but its results?

Well, they last for the rest of your life.

BE ENCOURAGED

I want to be sensitive here. You are graciously allowing me to enter a vulnerable space in your life. It's a place that may have been off limits for years to others, perhaps even to yourself. Understanding that, please allow me to encourage you.

You are about to break through—the torments that have plagued your life are about to cease. Therefore, don't be afraid. Take courage. God is with you! The Lord is going to help you to forgive yourself. So take these words to heart: "Have I not commanded you? Be strong and of good courage; do not be afraid, nor be dismayed, for the LORD your God is with you wherever you go" (Josh. 1:9).

You and I both know God is faithful to His promises. So as you take the steps to forgive yourself, you can be strong, courageous, and unafraid. God will help you, just as He helped Peter.

There was no one on earth who Peter loved more than he did Jesus. Peter loved Jesus so much that he willingly gave up everything he had—he even left his job to follow the Master. Jesus loved him deeply too. There were times Jesus allowed Peter to go places with Him that no other disciple was permitted to go. Jesus allowed Peter to see glimpses of His glory and to hear truth that only a few witnessed. Not only that, but Jesus uniquely gave Peter a powerful new name.

However, in spite of the love Jesus lavishly poured upon Peter, and the love Peter had for Jesus, Peter the Rock did the unimaginable. He committed an offense against Jesus he never thought in a million years he could do—he denied Jesus at the time of His greatest need.

When Jesus told Peter in advance that he would deny Him, Peter immediately and honestly replied that he'd die for Him before he would ever deny Him. And he truly meant it. Well, when the time came and Jesus was arrested, Peter failed him. He did not die with Jesus—he denied Jesus. He denied Jesus not once, not twice, but *three* times. These verses tell how Peter not only wounded Jesus but how he wounded himself.

Now Peter sat outside in the courtyard. And a servant girl came to him, saying, "You also were with Jesus of Galilee."

But he denied it before them all, saying, "I do not know what you are saying." And when he had gone out to the gateway, another girl saw him and said to those who were there, "This fellow also was with Jesus of Nazareth." But again he denied with an oath, "I do not know the Man!" And a little later those who stood by came up and said to Peter, "Surely you also are one of them, for your speech betrays you." Then he began to curse and swear, saying, "I do not know the Man!" Immediately a rooster crowed. And Peter remembered the word of Jesus who had said to him, "Before the rooster crows, you will deny me three times." So he went out and wept bitterly (Matt. 26:69–75).

Peter's bitter weeping indicates that the pain, remorse, and conviction he was experiencing was deep and traumatic. He was broken to the core of his being. He had committed a sin that he felt he was incapable of committing. The realization that he failed the One he loved more than anything on earth was unbearable. And it produced guilt within him that had the potential to destroy his life.

Peter faced a critical choice. Would he allow his terrible failure to destroy his life and destiny? Or would he choose to receive God's forgiveness and allow God's grace to empower him to forgive himself as well? We know from his two letters in the Bible and his powerful ministry in the book of Acts, Peter eventually forgave himself, but it took a healing discussion with Jesus in John 21:15–19 for that to begin to occur. Christ not only demonstrated His forgiveness but called Peter back into the ministry soon after his major failure. As Peter accepted Christ's full forgiveness, he also came to forgive himself. As you embrace the fact that upon your confession of your sin Christ also forgives you, you will be able to step right into the completion of the process by forgiving yourself.

The reason God placed these types of stories in the Bible is to encourage and help you and me. He wants us to know that if He could forgive Peter, and Peter could forgive himself, you and I can do the same. What better time is there than right now to prepare your heart to forgive yourself?

STAGE #1: PREPARING YOUR HEART TO FORGIVE YOURSELF

Like forgiving others, preparing your heart to forgive yourself requires two simple preparatory steps.

The first step in preparing yourself for this forgiveness is to make up your mind that you are going to forgive yourself for everything that yet remains unforgiven. If you are ready, please read the following out loud slowly, from your heart to confirm your decision:

I have decided of my own free will to forgive myself today for every wound I've given myself intentionally or accidentally and for wounding other people. I will fulfill the five requirements Jesus out-lined so that all heart infection and torment will completely end.

The next step will be to list on a piece of paper all the ways you have either wounded yourself or wounded other people including family, friends, coworkers, and strangers. When I have done this, I found the process difficult because I could no longer keep those painful words and actions stuffed away, out of my thoughts. What proved immensely motivating was the fact that I had learned the disastrous consequences that I would experience until I did forgive myself completely. I didn't want any torment to continue— not even one more day. Neither do you! It's a very small price to pay, our forgiveness, in comparison to the benefits that will happen as a result.

> Get a clean sheet of paper, as you did in an earlier chapter, and put your name on the top. Now list all the ways that you have wounded either yourself or those around you. As you think and write, pray for God to gently call to mind all those wounds—no matter how far in the past or painful—and to give you strength and peace as you prepare to forgive yourself.

Now let's get in touch with what's really going to happen. You are going to open your heart, extend compassion to yourself, release yourself from your heart-prison, forgive yourself for each of the wounds you caused yourself and others, and then bless yourself. To get ready, would you please say this sentence out loud?

I have decided of my own free will to forgive myself for all the painful wounds I have committed against myself or against others. I have held unforgiveness against myself long enough and choose to fully release myself from my heart-prison and forgive each and every trespass. No one and nothing shall hinder me from completing this in the next few moments. I want God's full approval due to my obedience and have lived long enough with this serious sin of unforgiveness. I will be free of all unforgiveness and torment, enjoying the full blessing of God in my life.

STAGE #2: TAKING THE STEPS

Remember, your heart is the place where the infection and the wound/s reside. It is the only spot where Jesus says forgiveness can truly take place. So for each step below you will find declarations in the form of key sentences to guide you to complete the necessary heart-work so that you will forgive. If you have already forgiven others, this will come quite easily.

The steps you are about to take will lead you to freedom. Each step involves you using your mind, your will, and most importantly—your heart. What this means is for every step you will decide (using your thoughts), choose (using your determination), and be open (using your heart) to allow yourself and the Spirit of God complete access to your heart.

Step 1: Open your heart to forgive yourself.

Chances are the door of your heart has been sealed shut for a long time now. When you locked the door you threw away the key in an attempt to squelch the pain caused by your internal suffering. However, you now understand that the tightly bolted door served only to keep pain in and healing out. But that's about to change! You are ready to take the first step to secure your freedom.

> Open the door of your heart by making the following declaration. Don't just say the words, but mean them. Say them slowly and allow those very words to actually open the door of your heart that has been shut for so long!
>
> *I hereby choose to not protect myself from my heart wounds that I have caused by hurting myself or others. I open my heart in order to forgive, set myself free, and end all torment.*

Is it opened? If not, try repeating those words again but more slowly, because sometimes doors that have been closed for a long time need an extra shove to pry open. Once you know that your heart is opened, by feeling peaceful certainty that you can move forward, move on to the next step.

Step 2: Extend compassion toward yourself.

The reason you have locked yourself in your heart-prison is because you lacked the mercy and compassion to forgive yourself initially. Now you must reverse that earlier decision, gather your determination and open your heart of compassion to the person you are going to forgive—yourself.

As hating yourself only results in unhealthy and damaging attitudes and actions, so balanced love for yourself only results in healthy and positive attitudes and actions.

But, an extremely important connection that directly affects your ability to forgive others and also forgive yourself is often missed. See if you identify with this all-important relationship we see in James 2:8–9: "If you really fulfill the royal law according to the Scripture, 'You shall love your neighbor as yourself,' you do well; but if you show partiality, you commit sin, and are convicted by the law as transgressors."

You are to love your neighbor in the same way you love yourself. What is abundantly clear is that the Bible teaches over and over again this same theme—you are to love yourself. This kind of love is not selfish or me-centered—it's the exact opposite.

If you don't love yourself, you will not be able to fulfill the will of God in your life. People with self-hatred always mistreat others. That's why people who don't forgive others will eventually slide into self-hatred, which makes it impossible to obey Christ and "love yourself."

In case you are thinking that loving yourself means becoming selfish and arrogant, you may be forgetting how the Bible describes true love in 1 Corinthians 13.

Love suffers long and is kind; love does not envy; love does not parade itself, is not puffed up; does not behave rudely, does not seek its own, is not provoked, thinks no evil; does not rejoice in iniquity, but rejoices in the truth; bears all things, believes all things, hopes all things, endures all things. (vv. 4–7)

If you are filled with these characteristics of love toward others and toward yourself, you will not have difficulties in extending love to others and also toward yourself. Will you fulfill the law of love and open your heart and love yourself the way God reveals is according to His will?

Stand outside yourself for a moment and look at yourself objectively. Do you hold back from truly loving yourself? This may be a new idea that might take some time to get used to, but it is one of the most powerful revelations in the Bible. It literally transforms a person.

In case you are still uncertain whether you should extend compassion to yourself, let's go one step further by reflecting on James 2:8–9 again: "If you really fulfill the royal law according to the Scripture, 'You shall love your neighbor as yourself,' you do well; but if you show partiality, you commit sin, and are convicted by the law as transgressors."

Verse 9 warns against showing partiality, which means we must not allow ourselves to show love to some and not to others. In fact, by showing partiality in this way, "you commit sin." It's sinful to not love everyone. But bring this concept back into the context of "love your neighbor *as yourself.*" The other person we seem to often miss loving is our self—you are not to show partiality to anyone by not extending compassion in love, or by showing partiality against yourself. If other people are to be loved and forgiven, then the person who is reading this sentence is also a person and must not be neglected or excluded. You must love yourself as the Bible teaches, or you will sin.

Take a look at the list you wrote earlier of the ways you wounded yourself. Now take the number one most difficult sin or mistake you have trouble forgiving yourself for and then answer these questions:

1. What was going on in my life when I injured others and myself?

2. Looking back over what I did, do I wish I acted differently?

3. Am I truly sorrowful and repentant for my actions?

4. Have others hurt me before? Did I extend compassion and mercy toward them?

5. As a person like everyone else who unfortunately makes painful mistakes and commits grievous sins from time to time, shouldn't I accept reality and choose to open my heart to give mercy and grace to myself?

As you work through each of these questions, the waters of mercy and compassion are now flowing into the dry and rough cracks of your heart. Now stop hesitating and fling open the floodgates and intentionally dive into the deep waters of God's mercy and compassion. Break open the dam by permitting yourself to both grant and accept your gift of compassion. Repeat and embrace the following key sentence:

I am not perfect, therefore I make mistakes and commit sins like everyone else. I choose to obey Christ and love myself by permitting myself to grant full mercy, grace, and compassion to myself. I accept reality and no longer deny what I did or deny my need to forgive myself.

Step 3: Release yourself from your inner heart-prison.

Anytime we choose not to forgive, a number of painful consequences inevitably occur. God responds by delivering us to the torturers and pulling back the protective boundaries of our peace. We respond to what we have done by chaining ourselves to the walls of our inner heart-prison. As Jesus revealed, we bind ourselves due to the debt we feel for what we did either to ourselves or others. Until that debt is paid, we erroneously feel that we suffer for the suffering we caused—thus we remain locked up in that secret dungeon of our heart, day after day, year after year.

We describe this tragedy in various ways such as "I built walls around my heart" or "I just couldn't forgive myself." Because of those walls and dungeon bars, you began that inevitable slide into deeper and deeper torments of self-bitterness, self-slander, self-resentment, self-hatred, and ultimately self-vengeance. Never lose sight of the fact that no one has the power to stop that destructive slide. As time passes, those wounds will spread and you will inevitably and sadly demonstrate all seven characteristics of the unforgiven.

Whether or not you have ever considered this before, your heart knows who is locked within. How deeply your heart longs for freedom, but only you have the key. Prayer, Bible reading, church attendance, and acts of service will not release you. No other key will ever work, no matter how hard or how long you may try. Only your forgiveness will unlock this door.

The longer we remain locked in our dank cell, the greater our inner anxiety and distress. We learn to cope by hardening our heart to endure the pain and distress. Instead of a tender and open heart to others and ourselves, we wrestle with apathy, passivity, turmoil, and anxiety. Aren't you tired of fighting these beasts? Don't you long for those days when you were emotionally alive and vibrant? Then turn that door handle and start down those stairs with a sense of release and joyful anticipation.

Your compassion is now aligned with God's commands. It is time for you to reenter that prison in your heart, but this time all the cells will be empty, except for one—yours. To free yourself from your own inner prison, imagine this as vividly as you can:

You open the door to your heart-prison and make your way back down the rocky stairwell. You feel heavy. Sad. You have suffered much in this neglected place. Still, you smile as you pass the now-empty cells that previously held all those who wounded you. Those iron doors lie on the floor, ripped off their hinges when you decided to never again use those cells of unforgiveness. The further you walk, the lighter your heart becomes. You remember their joy when you set them free. You start running. You cannot wait to let the last person you love out of this terrible place—yourself.

You walk over to the cell and see yourself looking down, feeling shame and rejection, remembering what you had done to "deserve" this. You mourn for the lost years, sobbing from sorrow, full of repentance. You are so sorry for what you did.

Then you cry to yourself, the last prisoner, "I am so sorry! I release you!"

The prisoner walks free. You embrace. And at that moment, you both become one. The "other" becomes "you" again. Instead of brokenness and isolation and anger, bitterness, resentment, slander, hatred, and vengeance toward that "you" in the prison, now all that remains is freedom and joy. You have been restored!

Tears flow as you dance back up those stairs. Your joy cannot be contained. You are free, free at last. Your heart now is released fully toward God, and you burst into praise to the Lord for His gracious love and acceptance.

Now make it official—so that every tormentor and everything that has been associated with your captivity knows that those days are soon over, including the legal contract—because you are now going to forgive yourself for each wound. Embrace these words making the declaration:

I hereby open the doors of my heart-prison and release myself. I no longer hold myself in contempt for what I did. I accept reality—and no longer deny what I did or judge myself for it. My heart-prison is finally and forever empty— and I am now full!

Step 4: Forgive yourself for each wound.

You have released yourself. Enjoy the warmth of the sunshine of freedom for a moment. Then look over at that rock where your acts or attitudes that caused the wounds are piled. You know that you aren't equal to what you have done. You are separate from your actions. All of them occurred in the past and you are alive in the present.

Think of your life as a huge white poster with a few small and large X's scrawled on various places. The vast majority of your life poster is pure and unmarred! Don't allow any condemnation or accusation to raise its ugly head. You are now ready to erase those X's off your life poster until it's pure and forgiven once again. So take out your eraser and walk over with full intention to not leave even one area unforgiven. Erase away!

Now it is time to forgive yourself for each and every wound, one at a time. Take that piece of paper that you've used to list all the wounds you must forgive yourself. You know this is going to be easier than the first time because your heart is now rushing to complete this. You know how close you are to freedom.

To forgive yourself, go through each of your wounds one at a time. As you did before, start with the most difficult first, then go through the list one by one. Read through the statements below for the number one wound and then repeat until you know all the wounds have been cleansed and healing has begun.

- "I've decided to forgive myself for each and every wound."

- "I've had unforgiveness toward myself for far too long and that is ending right now."

- "I have opened my heart and released myself from prison, and now I'm going to give myself a wonderful gift of my complete forgiveness."

- "I forgive myself for the wound of _____." *(Name the hardest wound to forgive.)*

- "From my heart, I genuinely forgive myself for the wound of _____" *(same wound as above).*

- *Slowly now*—"With all of my heart, I fully and completely forgive myself for the wound of _____" *(same wound as above). Do that one more time.*

- "I fully forgive myself for _____ (same wound as above) and no longer hold it against myself."

You are actually forgiving yourself. You may need to restate those same confessions again if you know you haven't yet forgiven yourself from your heart. Don't run from this process. Instead state them one more time, *slowly*, and from your heart. Having done this a number of times in my own life and having helped so many over the years, I know we often need to give ourselves a little grace while our heart fully embraces forgiveness.

Now go through the same process with the second hardest wound to forgive. By this point, you will be able to forgive all the wounds on the entire list. Just use this sentence and fill in the next wound, and the next wound, and so on, until you have gone through them all.

"From my heart, I genuinely forgive myself for the wound of _____" (describe the wound).

When you are finished with the list, you may be wondering if you remembered them all. As before, use The Forgiveness Validator. State out loud, from your heart:

"Before God, I have forgiven myself for everything."

Again, be still and wait before God. Anticipate God will prompt regarding other wounds that you missed. Use the same process until God no longer reveals any additional trespasses and you sense His peace.

Step 5: Bless and do good to yourself.

Did this step come as a surprise to you? Does the thought of blessing yourself seem odd and a bit out of place? It shouldn't. What sense does it make for us to bless and seek to do good to someone we forgave and yet exclude ourselves from that list? You have great reason to celebrate!

Throughout the Bible, various people prayed that God would bless them. In fact, God instructs religious leaders to ask that God bless their own people. As the New Testament clearly reveals, "you do not have because you do not ask" (James 4:2). Don't you want the Lord to pour out His full and abundant blessings now that you have fully obeyed Him and He has canceled the contract of your discipline? He awaits only one thing—your prayer.

Consider this concept—"you do not have because you do not ask." The protocol of this type of blessing is simple: ask for God to bless you abundantly for His purposes. If you're familiar with my book *The Prayer of Jabez*, this won't be new to you—and now would be a great time to ask God to bless you anew. Everywhere I travel in the world, people tell me powerful stories of what happened in their lives when they asked God to bless them abundantly and expand their ministry to others. You will rarely have a moment like this one, my friend, where you have broken through at such a significant level. So, don't hesitate even for another moment. Call out to God:

> Dear Lord,
>
> How I thank You for Your loving discipline in bringing me to the point that I have forgiven everyone else and myself! I also thank You that I have been able, by Your grace, to completely forgive everyone, including myself, so that You cancel and annul all forms of torment caused by my unforgiveness. As disobedience brings discipline, so also obedience brings blessings.
>
> Will You now show Your pleasure for my actions by pouring out upon me abundant blessings, overflowing blessings from Your kind hand of compassion? I praise Your holy name. In Jesus' name. Amen.

STAGE #3: RECEIVING GOD'S GRACIOUS FORGIVENESS

Before leaving this chapter, one final action yet remains—a prayer of repentance for the sins you committed while you remained in unforgiveness toward yourself:

Dear God,

I confess to You my sins of unforgiveness toward myself, anger, bitterness against myself, slander, resentment, self-hatred, and the desire for self-vengeance—to try to make myself pay for my sins and mistakes. I accept the fact that Christ paid for my sins. I now realize I have suffered needlessly by practicing vengeance upon myself for my sins and mistakes. Please forgive me and cleanse me from all unrighteousness. Please forgive me as I no longer have unforgiveness in my life. In Jesus' name, Amen.

Well, congratulations my friend.

If you've done and lived out this book, not just read it, then you've walked a remarkable path. Your heart is open. You hold no one hostage to your unforgiveness.

God smiles at what you've done today.

And your heart, made from the beginning for so much, for love and peace and joy and openness, well, your heart is *ready*.

Ready to live in freedom.

"Today I opened my heart, extended compassion, released myself from my heart-prison, forgave all my self-inflicted wounds, and blessed myself!"

Signature: _____

Date: _____

CHAPTER ELEVEN

The Secret of Lasting Forgiveness

THE VIBRANT HOPE OF A FORGIVING LIFE

> "Forgiveness says you are given another chance
> to make a new beginning."
>
> —DESMOND TUTU

What a journey this has been.

You are to be commended! Forgiving can be difficult at times. Opening the doors of your heart-prison and freeing the people who wounded you, including yourself, can be draining. Emotionally exhausting. Chances are, while working through your forgiveness process, a tear or two may even have fallen on the pages of this book. Or, you may have experienced a wide range of unexpected emotions as you forgave wounds from the past. But you have overcome and courageously obeyed the command of Jesus and have forgiven others and yourself.

So exhale.

Now inhale.

Fill your lungs with fresh air and hope.

Years ago, I was at a conference hosted by a national Christian organization at a ski resort in Colorado. The director came up to me with some of the older staff members. "Will you help us?" he asked. "We have a crisis on our hands. One of our staff members has been deeply traumatized and can barely speak. We've been trying for weeks to help, but I'm afraid that we're losing her."

"What happened?" I asked.

The story they told me was horrible.

One Saturday afternoon around two o'clock, the young woman drove to the local grocery store. After pulling into one of the parking spaces, she turned off the ignition, exited her car, and locked the door. And the unimaginable happened. Four men jumped out of a car next to her and attacked her. She tried to run away. They grabbed her, knocked her to the ground, and raped her one by one, in a parking lot in broad daylight. No one came to answer her screams for help.

I was shaken, angered. And the thought surged in my heart—her life can't be ruined by this. God wants her to find freedom again.

After the evening session, the young woman and I sat down together. We weren't strangers—she'd attended this conference several times before when I'd spoken. It was obvious that she was tortured inside from the horrific trauma she'd endured. After a few moments of catching up, I asked her, "May I talk openly with you?" She nodded.

"This wasn't your fault," I said.

We talked as friends, until she understood the pain she was experiencing was not hers alone. God shared her pain. His heart was close to hers. He lamented the injustice she'd suffered. And His presence was near to her—ready to bring comfort and healing.

It took time, but she finally embraced the truth that she was innocent, not in *any* way responsible for what had happened. There was no guilt that she should carry, no matter what the lying voices inside her said.

I believe that healing can only occur with sensitive honesty, not avoidance. Her thoughts needed to be vocalized. So, I continued, "You have a few options at this point in your life. You could decide to hate your attackers—perhaps even hate all men. You can live in that hatred for the rest of your life." She didn't say anything, but nodded slowly in agreement.

"Furthermore, you could listen to the lies that I'm sure are whispering in your heart—you could begin to believe that you are 'damaged goods,' that your worth as a person has been stolen. You could run from your values to promiscuity, trying to numb your pain. After all, those lies say, no one is going to want you, so why not?" She nodded. "Have thoughts like that ever crossed your mind?" I asked her.

She looked down but nodded again. "Yes, they have."

"And, through all of this, you could shut your heart against anyone who wanted to get close to you. To protect your heart, you could reject every man because you believe the lie that no one would ever want you. Some of your deepest hopes have been ruthlessly taken away from you, haven't they?" We wept together.

The truth sets one free, no matter how painful it is.

Finally, she was prepared to move towards healing, so I said, "there's another way, another option."

"What's the other way?" she asked.

I steadied my heart. "You can rise up and overcome it."

You could see in her eyes that she in no way believed that was possible.

"You did not have any control over what happened to you," I continued. "But you have full control over what you do from this point forward. God can redeem even this. Although that may sound impossible or terribly naive to you, do not lose confidence in our great God. He hates what they did to you and loves you with overwhelming compassion.

"So," I began to ask her, "would you like to know how to follow in the footsteps of others who rose up and overcame their trauma?" She nodded again, and I saw hope flicker.

"This will be most difficult," I said. "For God's full blessing, and your freedom from ongoing torment, God asks you to give a gift to the most undeserving people. You are invited to grant forgiveness to those four men."

Her eyes flashed. Their message was clear—those four men do not deserve to be forgiven—they deserve the worst kind of punishment.

I nodded in agreement. "They deserve the most severe punishment and you deserve complete justice. But forgiveness is different than justice. The police will catch them. Justice will be fulfilled. But the only option you have is to release and forgive them or remain chained to these painful memories with anger, bitterness, hatred, and vengeance—all dominating your life until you forgive."

She was faced with what must have been the most difficult decision of her life.

Years passed. I was in the Midwest speaking to a large group of college students. At the end of our week together, there was a lot of buzzing and giggling going on. Two people who everybody in the group loved were going to announce their engagement. They had planned a big celebration—with cake, balloons, and the whole works.

I stood off in the wings because I didn't know them. Then the couple came forward, beaming. There was so much excitement. I got caught up in the moment and contributed my fair share of claps and hoorahs. I was so happy for them.

When the celebration finished I returned to the podium to get my notes. Standing there was the celebrated couple. The young woman turned to me. "You don't remember me."

I said, "No ma'am, I don't. I'm so sorry."

She said, "I was the girl who was raped four times. This is the man of my dreams! I chose to forgive the men who violated me, and God has given me victory and beauty in my life. And I am so happy now."

A miracle had happened. Victory and freedom came to overcome incredible darkness. By God's grace she rose up and overcame—she forgave.

And if she can forgive—moving into abundant life and joy—well, I think that I can.

And I think that you can too.

In forgiveness we enter a new way of living—a life of freedom.

When you forgave, you entered a life filled with vibrant hope, overflowing with God's peace. Things will be different now—much different.

How?

Prior to forgiving, you were a prisoner who kept prisoners. You were chained by your unforgiveness, holding others in captivity, tormented. Your mind was bombarded daily by unwanted thoughts, all while you wished your wounds would heal and your pain would go away. You felt yourself becoming a person you didn't recognize as you slid down The Slide of Unforgiveness.

But you are a prisoner no longer. Your story now is freedom.

Throughout the book we have shared stories of people who are just like you and me. People who broke out of prisons of unforgiveness and found freedom and peace.

There are so many other stories I could tell from years of ministry. Stories from all over the world where people of all skin tones, all backgrounds, found peace once they forgave. All of these people's stories changed to stories of freedom, peace, and hope. Their life stories were rewritten. Unforgiveness had snuffed out their hope, but forgiveness reignited it. Their lives changed—not always to become lives of ease, but to become lives full of joy and love.

Now a new story is emerging—yours.

I don't know your situation. But I do know the torment related to unforgiveness has ceased because you have forgiven like God has forgiven us. Your life is going to be dramatically different. Your heart is open. Just as we discovered how the hidden connection of unforgiveness affects your entire life negatively. You're on the path to discover in the days ahead how forgiving can affect your entire life positively.

A forgiving life is a life of vibrant, expectant hope.

This is the way of life Jesus has always intended for you. Yes, He understands the painful wounds of sin and injustice we experience in life. However, He made it crystal clear—choosing to forgive ourselves and others is always the right choice to make. To be like Him. To be like the Father.

Finally, remember, God desires freedom and peace for your life—for you to live the joyous way He intended. And the way to continually abide in His peace and freedom is to forgive and keep on forgiving. A beautiful way of living modeled and taught to us by His Son, Jesus Christ.

May God richly bless you, and may you continually enjoy the peace and freedom flowing from a life of forgiveness!

We hope this book has led you toward forgiveness, freedom, and peace. And we hope you find someone to share in your joy! We would be excited to hear your story of forgiveness and transformation; if you'd like to share it with us, visit teacheverynation.org/mystory.

In reading *The Secret of Lasting Forgiveness*, some of you may find yourselves confronting deep pain and trauma from your past. If so, we encourage you to reach out to someone who can help you process those things and find healing. We've compiled a list of resources and contacts to help get you started; you can find it at www.zealbooks.com/the-secret-of-lasting-forgiveness-resources.

PUBLISHERS GUARANTEE

This is our guarantee for buyers of *The Secrets of Lasting Forgiveness:* If you have read this book in its entirety and followed all of the steps in each chapter, you will find peace when you forgive others and yourself.

If you don't experience peace, we will send you a check* within 30 days of receiving your correspondence. (See details below.)]

My name is _____
and I didn't experience the peace you guaranteed.

(You must mark all boxes below to receive a refund.)

In checking these boxes, I certify:

_____ I purchased this book for myself.

_____ I read 100% of *The Secret of Lasting Forgiveness*.

_____ I followed all of the steps outlined by Dr. Wilkinson to forgive others.

_____ I followed all of the steps outlined by Dr. Wilkinson to forgive myself.

Please fill in your mailing address below:

Name: _____

Address: _____

City: _____ State: _____ Zip: _____

Phone: _____

You must cut out this page and the front cover of* The Secret of Lasting Forgiveness *and mail both of them to:

Zeal Books, PO Box 80945, Portland, OR 97280

*The check amount will be for the 30 day average listed sales price of the book on Amazon.

ACKNOWLEDGMENTS

It would take pages and pages to fit the names of everyone who made a difference in the development of this book. Therefore, please consider this a sincere but incomplete expression of my gratitude.

This book never would have seen the light of day without the relentless encouragement from my lifelong friend Don Jacobson, who has also been my primary publisher for many years. He and his wife Brenda heard me share the contents of this book at a Teach Every Nation Board Meeting, and the message so impacted them that they immediately encouraged me to turn it into a book. For over 18 months, Don pursued his vision through telephone calls, emails, and texts. Finally, I knew it couldn't be postponed any longer. Thank you, Don and Brenda, and to their new publishing company, Zeal Books!

Don's expertise wasn't just in convincing me to write the book. He also suggested Mark Strong as a co-writer, and it quickly became apparent that he was exactly the right man for the job. Mark put all these truths from my mind and heart into a most readable fashion. We spent two extensive but exhilarating long weekends together, brainstorming and outlining each chapter of *The Secret of Lasting Forgiveness*, discussing, praying, rewriting, and editing. Without Mark's heart, writing skills, creativity, and commitment to the message, the book could never have developed into what it is now. Thank you, Mark! May we write many others together in the future, my friend.

Zeal put together an amazing team of people who all helped create and shape this book. Paul Pastor, a highly gifted wordsmith and editor, honed the book to an even greater level of readability and excellence. His contribution cannot be overestimated. Thank you, Paul! Jason Gabbert is an award winning graphics designer who designed the cover. Thank you, Jason, for your creativity and innovation. To the eighteen readers who offered the editorial team invaluable feedback and suggestions: your comments helped the book to be more clear, concise, and compelling. Thanks to each of you! Clarke Leland of Cascadiom Media filmed the book trailer that so beautifully captured the spirit of *The Secret of Lasting Forgiveness*. I was moved as I watched his portrayal. Thank you, Clarke! Thanks also to Scott Erickson, who painted the incredible visual representation of the book featured in the video; thank you for lending your artistic gifts. Martin Raz, Zeal's highly skilled Director of Operations, was behind the scenes making everything come together. Thank you, "Raz"—you developed the vision into reality!

Throughout the entire process, my precious wife, Darlene, stood by me—encouraging, praying, and granting much grace as I stayed riveted to my laptop weekend after weekend. She read various versions, always with a word of encouragement and insight. Her advice quietly shaped the manuscript. Thank you, Sweetheart!

Finally, I cannot complete this page without publicly confessing the greatest sin for any writer: I stole the content. I must admit that every big idea was His. And every story in the book included His personal involvement. I guess you could say, at least partially, anyway, the only truly original part of this book is this acknowledgments page. Everything else belongs to Jesus. Only Jesus. Gratitude and acknowledgment are just too shallow a response. Maybe that's why I'll be singing His praise forever and ever. ~ Bruce

To my wife, Marla, who has stuck it out with me through the thick and the thin, the bad days and the goods ones and every other in between. You are awesome! ~ Mark

BRUCE WILKINSON

Dr. Bruce Wilkinson is an international ministry leader and the #1 *New York Times* bestselling author of over sixty books, including *The Prayer of Jabez*. Bruce's books have been translated into thirty languages and include the NYT bestsellers *Secrets of the Vine* and *A Life God Rewards*, as well as *The Dream Giver*. Other favorites include *You Were Born for This!*, *The 7 Laws of the Learner*, *Experiencing Spiritual Breakthroughs*, *Set Apart*, *My 100 Best-Loved Bible Stories* (the bestselling Children's Bible in Africa), and *Talk Through the Bible*, which he wrote with Ken Boa.

His ministry ranges from packed stadiums to counseling over coffee, from trusted Bible teaching to leading a major African AIDS education initiative, Beat the Drum. Bruce founded Never-Ending Gardens, a movement that planted over 1,100,000 vegetable gardens for orphans and widows in Africa; founded the widely respected Walk Thru the Bible Ministries; was chairman and co-founder of the CoMission to the former Soviet Union; and has led national reconciliation meetings in Uganda, Namibia, and South Africa. Bruce is currently the chairman of Teach Every Nation, a Bible training movement educating tens of thousands of church leaders who cannot access or afford traditional academic institutions. He is also the founder and chairman of The Exponential Group, which has raised over $65,000,000 for nonprofit organizations. He is happily married to Darlene. They have three children, David, Jennifer, and Jessica, and eleven grandchildren—ten boys and only one girl! They live in South Carolina.

MARK STRONG

Dr. Mark E. Strong is a pastor and author. He and his wife, Marla, have served as the senior pastors of Life Change Church, a dynamic and diverse church located in the heart of Portland, Oregon, since 1988. Life Change is the same church where Mark first came to faith in Christ, and Mark now leads the community as they labor for personal, social, and spiritual transformation in their city and community. He is a gifted communicator who has preached and taught the Bible throughout the United States and the world, following his passion to build the church and help people find freedom and grow in their relationship with Christ. Mark holds a BA in speech communications from Portland State University, an MA in biblical studies from Western Evangelical Seminary, and a Doctorate of Ministry Leadership from George Fox Evangelical Seminary, where he now serves on the Board of Regents. He is the author of *Church for the Fatherless*, *The Divine Merger*, and *The Blessing Maker*. Mark and Marla have been married for thirty years and have four children.

UNLOCK THE SECRETS TO UNDERSTANDING GOD'S WORD
WITH ONE OF THE WORLD'S FOREMOST BIBLE TEACHERS

Do you find the Bible confusing? Are you searching to understand its message and meaning? The Bible is the world's most popular book, but at the same time the most misunderstood!

Yet understanding the Bible is the key to discovering God's plan for your life and helping others to grow spiritually. And God wants you to hear and comprehend His story.

Rekindle your passion for God in a creative way that connects your head, heart, and hands. Join us for the newest course from Teach Every Nation and world-class Bible teacher, Bruce Wilkinson.

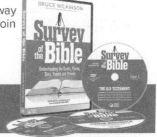

"Survey of the Bible: Understanding the Books, Places, Story, People and Periods". An Exciting New 8-Part, Bible-based Video Curriculum.

BRUCEWILKINSONCOURSES.ORG/SURVEY

STOP WISHING YOU WERE SOMEONE ELSE AND DISCOVER WHO YOU WERE BORN TO BE

Escape the Ordinary is a dynamic, new Bible-based video curriculum from best-selling author and teacher, Bruce Wilkinson.

Based on his groundbreaking book, *You Were Born for This*, Bruce will lead you to embrace the extraordinary by volunteering for divine assignments. He explores from Scripture how you were born to fulfill God's very specific plan and purpose. And he reveals how God has already equipped you with the skills necessary to complete the assignments He sends you on. In the process, you will discover how God is present and active in your daily life.

When God knocks on your door, what do you do? In his creative, story-driven, highly motivating style, Bruce will show you how you can learn the "protocol of heaven" to "open the door" and experience miracles.

Escape the Ordinary.
Informative.
Motivating.
LifeChanging.

You will never
be the same.

BRUCEWILKINSONCOURSES.ORG/ESCAPE

THE FATHER-SHIFT CONFERENCE

Millions of people across our nation and around the world are painfully impacted by the epidemic of fatherlessness. In America alone, 24.7 million children (33%) lived in a home without their biological father in 2010. Another 20.3 million lived with no father (biological, adoptive, or stepfather) in the home. This means one out of every three children in our nation has no father presence in their lives.

In addition to the many fatherless children in our nation, there are many adults who carry the pain of a father-wound, whether it was caused by an absent father or an incompetent father.

Something has to change!

Father-Shift is a dynamic conference designed to change lives by:

1. Sharing the love of an always present and faithful Father-God.

2. Facilitating conversations in churches and communities about fatherlessness.

3. Bringing healing to men and women suffering from the pain of a father-wound.

4. Empowering men to be good fathers.

5. Encouraging men to serve the fatherless around them.

If you would like to know more about Father-Shift, or would like to host a conference, contact us at fathershift.org, or follow us on twitter at @markestrong.

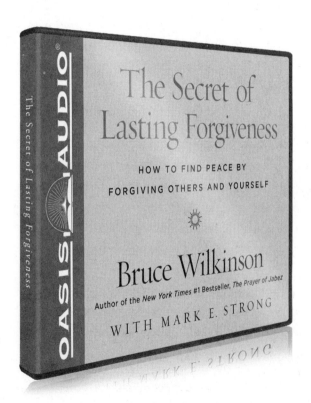

ZEALbooks

Portland, Oregon

Zeal Books is a new publisher dedicated to world-changing ideas. We're focused and founded on love—love for our authors and love for their books. And love makes you zealous. Zeal's commitment to its authors, readers, and accounts is to only publish books we're zealous for—books the world needs.

Visit us online for news, resources, and more at zealbooks.com, or find us on social media:

🐦 @ZealBks

 @ZealBks

 facebook.com/zealbks